LANZA
HIS TRAGIC LIFE

LANZA
HIS TRAGIC LIFE

RAYMOND STRAIT
&TERRY ROBINSON

PRENTICE-HALL, INC., ENGLEWOOD CLIFFS, N.J.

Lanza: His Tragic Life
by Raymond Strait and Terry Robinson
Copyright © 1980 by Raymond Strait and Terry Robinson
All rights reserved. No part of this book may be
reproduced in any form or by any means, except
for the inclusion of brief quotations in a review,
without permission in writing from the publisher.
Address inquiries to Prentice-Hall, Inc.,
Englewood Cliffs, N.J. 07632
Printed in the United States of America
Prentice-Hall International, Inc., London
Prentice-Hall of Australia, Pty. Ltd., Sydney
Prentice-Hall of Canada, Ltd., Toronto
Prentice-Hall of India Private Ltd., New Delhi
Prentice-Hall of Japan, Inc., Tokyo
Prentice-Hall of Southeast Asia Pte. Ltd., Singapore
Whitehall Books Limited, Wellington, New Zealand

10 9 8 7 6 5 4 3 2 1

Library of Congress Cataloging in Publication Data

Strait, Raymond.
Lanza, his tragic life.
Includes index.
1. Lanza, Mario, 1921–1959. 2. Singers—United
States—Biography. I. Robinson, Terry, date
joint author. II. Title.
ML420.L24S8   784'.092'4 [B]   80-17281
ISBN 0-13-523407-7

Dedicated to . . .

*Colleen, Ellisa, Damon, and Marc Lanza—for allowing
us to tell the private and public life of their
parents as it really was, so that somehow, somewhere,
someone may profit from their experiences.*

*To Mark and Russell Strait for the constant
disruption of their lives while it was being written.*

*And especially to Sylvia for endurance
beyond the call of duty.*

We love you all—

"Uncle" Terry Robinson and Raymond Strait

CONTENTS

I

It was 1921. The *Boston Post* won a Pulitzer Prize for journalism; Warren G. Harding became the twenty-ninth President of the United States, and the New York Giants beat Babe Ruth and the Yankees 5 games to 3 in the World Series. It was the year the great Italian tenor, Enrico Caruso, died and, comparatively unnoticed, Alfredo Arnold Cocozza was born on January 31 at the home of his maternal grand-parents in South Philadelphia, Pennsylvania.

He was baptized by a priest named Caruso while his father and mother looked on, and without fanfare became another Catholic Italian-American baby on the ledger of the parish church. Maria (his mother) was 17 and Antonio (his father) was 10 years her senior. Alfredo would eventually adopt his mother's first and maiden names to become Mario Lanza.

The first grandchild born to Salvatore Lanza, a grocery importer and merchant, was cause for celebration in the Italian quarter of South Philadelphia. Salvatore had come to America from Abruzzi, Italy. His wife brought Maria a short time later when she was a six-month-old baby. Salvatore sold vegetables along the Philadelphia Main Line from his horse and wagon, getting up long before daylight to supply his regular customers and eventually earning enough money to buy a house and open a store. He and his wife lived with all eight of their children above the store, which still stands on Christian Street.

Alfred entered the world at 9:45 on a cold and windy

Monday morning. He was a blond baby, which was unusual since both parents had jet black hair. When the doctor left the Lanza home following the delivery, word spread through the neighborhood: "It's a boy!" For hours afterward people came and went and there was a party to celebrate the event.

Freddie, as the young Lanza was called, spent his early years in a crowded house that included not only his parents and grandparents, but five aunts and two uncles, plus occasional visiting cousins. Tony, who had been permanently disabled as a soldier in World War I and was on a government pension, stayed home with him while Mary went to work in a shirt factory. (They had Americanized their given names.)

The Italian neighborhood Freddie grew up in provided a rich ethnic experience. The church bells announcing mass often caught him playing stickball in the street, reminding him that he was supposed to be serving as altar boy and would probably get another lecture on punctuality from the priest. From the age of four, he would sit on the curb in front of Salvatore's store, listening to opera records being played in the music store a few doors away. His mother, whose own hopes for a career in grand opera had been dampened by Salvatore's male chauvinism, encouraged her son's interest.

Although Freddie was an altar boy in St. Mary Magdalena de Pazzi Church, the first Catholic Church in South Philadelphia, he was far from being an angel. A natural athlete and a born leader, he grew up a sturdy, adventurous boy, with hair that was finally turning black.

When Freddie was only nine he got a taste of violence close to home. Returning home from an errand for his mother, he found a crowd outside the house. He pushed through it and saw the bullet-riddled corpse of his father's brother, Uncle Vincent Cocozza, lying in a pool of blood. It was a gangland shooting but the details were hazy and, as usual in such incidents, nobody admitted to witnessing it.

Not long afterward, Mary decided it was time she and Tony had their own home. They moved to a two-story house at 20th and Mercy streets. Down the street was a record shop owned by a man named Petrella and it became a hangout for Freddie.

Even as a boy he could quote from any opera. The older men loved to get him into heated arguments about operatic music. He was so adept at presenting his case in these debates that his mother had hopes of his becoming a lawyer.

She didn't neglect his musical talent either. Mary introduced him to the violin but he disliked it so much he tossed it out the window, and she found it the next morning splintered in the yard. Undaunted, she bought him a player pianola, and later a piano, and found a music teacher for him. Freddie would put opera records on the Victrola, pick out the notes, and play them by ear.

America had entered the Great Depression. Freddie spent his summers at Salvatore's summer house in Wildwood, New Jersey. By the time he was fifteen he was a handsome, husky young man and girls were high on his priority list. His mother continued all her life to see only the altar boy and remain blind to his wilder side.

Later in life Terry Robinson asked Lanza how he could sing as he did. His response was, "It's all sex, Terry. When I'm singing, I'm scoring. That's me. It comes right out of my balls." At Wildwood he scored in a more literal way. He always had to be first with every girl, ahead of his friends. It was a rule: Freddie gets the girl first.

From the beginning his mother was so devoted to him that she refused to believe anything bad of her son. They were inseparable. As he grew into his teens, the age span between them seemed less because Mary continued to retain her sweet-sixteen figure and looks. He loved to hear her sing and would sit for hours and listen as she sang the arias he loved. They took long walks and went shopping together. Once, as they strolled down the street, some boys in front of a drugstore ogled Mary and one of the young men made an amorous remark. After a few steps Freddie asked his mother to walk on ahead. "I just want to see one of the guys for a minute. I'll catch up with you." Leaving Mary, he ran back to the fellow,

3

smashed him in the mouth, and knocked him down. "That's my mother," he warned. "Next time I'll finish you for good!"

Mary encouraged him to box. "Be a man," she said. "Don't let anybody push you around." But she forbade him to play football, fearing he might be seriously injured. He played anyway—without her knowledge.

Salvatore doted on his grandson, although he tried not to let his affection interfere with his sense of what was good for the boy. At Wildwood Freddie was in the habit of staying out late. One night his grandfather waited up for him. As he tiptoed into the house, Salvatore faced him sternly. "No more late hours," he ordered. "You be in bed by ten o'clock."

Several nights later Freddie came home earlier than usual. Salvatore looked up from his paper. "What's the matter? You sick? It is only nine o'clock."

"No, Grandpa," he was told, "I'm tired tonight. I'm going upstairs and go to bed."

Salvatore nodded and smiled.

Freddie went up to his room, put some pillows under the covers, climbed down the tree by his window, and went off to join his pals. About four-thirty in the morning there was a rainstorm. Salvatore got up, closed the windows, and went outside to tie down some of his plants against the wind. Just then he heard someone coming up the street and whistling a tune; he looked up to see his grandson sauntering along in the downpour.

"Where have you been?" he asked.

Freddie thought quickly.

"Oh, I went down to the station to pick up your paper so you wouldn't get wet."

"Then where is the paper?"

"The train didn't come in yet, so no paper." He scooted into the house leaving his grandfather scratching his head.

The future Mario Lanza was already showing the strengths and weaknesses that would make him a charismatic personality: a bit of a hell-raiser, charming, spoiled (especially by his mother), hot-tempered, a lady's man who prided himself

4

on his personal appearance and who was popular with the boys for his leadership and athletic ability—but who also had (the one thing his male friends couldn't fathom) an intense love of music and opera. In music appreciation class he was called on to lecture to the class on opera and the teacher recognized with some embarrassment that Freddie knew more about music than she did.

His quick temper got the best of him one day in school. A male teacher made the mistake of calling him a *wop* in class. Without thinking, Freddie belted the man, an act which promptly got him suspended. In spite of his parents' pleas he was not allowed to return to South Philadelphia High School and was transferred to Lincoln Prep.

At Lincoln, Freddie joined the school chorus, which consisted of twenty or so boys and girls plus the instructor. They often entertained at neighborhood functions, but there was nothing really to indicate that he was considering a singing career. He was not a featured singer in the group; he never sang a lead. Besides, Mary still had her heart set on his becoming a lawyer.

One day during his senior year she asked him, "Freddie, it's getting close to graduation. Have you thought about what you're going to do after high school? Maybe college?"

He looked at his mother, hesitated, and grinned. "Mom, what I want to be will cost a lot of money. Maybe more money even than going to college."

Ambition was something Mary liked. "What do you want to be that is so expensive?"

"I want to be a singer."

Mary was a little taken aback but not for long. "All right," she said, "we shall see about it."

She found a well-known baritone, Antonio Scarduzzo, who was coaching in South Philadelphia, and made arrangements for him to hear Freddie. She wanted an expert's opinion. There was no use wasting money if Freddie showed no promise. She was certain this was just a phase he was going through.

While Mary and Tony waited in the front parlor, Scarduzzo took Freddie into his music room. Soon they heard a beautiful tenor voice emanating from the room. Mary turned to her husband and said, "Mr. Scarduzzo must be finishing up a singing lesson with one of his advanced pupils."

"Yes," Tony said, "it's a beautiful voice. I wonder who it belongs to?"

"I don't know, but I hope Freddie will be next," Mary said. "I know he's nervous. Maybe his voice will dry up and he won't be able to sing."

A few moments later Scarduzzo emerged with his arm around Freddie's waist. They were both smiling.

"Maestro," Tony asked, "who was singing when you took our Freddie back into the room with you? Was it anybody we know?"

Scarduzzo looked at Mary and Tony and beamed. "There was no one else. You didn't know?"

Mary and Tony shook their heads in confusion.

"It was your own son!" He explained Freddie's great natural talent, but he cautioned all of them about his youth and the dangers inherent in too much training too soon. "He is young," the teacher said, "and you should not give him singing lessons. Not yet. Wait until he's about nineteen for that. Plenty of time. For the moment he should study languages, music, piano, and *solfeggio* (sight-reading of music)."

Mary's mind raced faster than the trolley they were riding home. Suddenly the future was focused entirely on Freddie's voice. She spoke seriously to her son, seeing him in a light she had never seen him in before. "You *will* have your lessons, Freddie. You will study hard. You can have *my* career. *You* will be the singer of the family."

During the ride home from Scarduzzo's studio she figured everything out. She was employed in the Quartermaster Corps and Tony was receiving 100 percent disability payments. It was not enough. No matter, she would take a second job as a waitress; she knew of an opening. Freddie would be *Maria Lanza* if she couldn't. She smiled to herself, patted her purse, and gazed out the window as the trolley rattled along the street.

In close-knit South Philadelphia's Italian colony it didn't take long for the community to become aware of the "singing genius" in the Cocozza family.

Freddie was placed in the hands of Mario Pellizon, a language teacher, three days a week for lessons in Italian, French, and German, his mother taking responsibility for the Neapolitan dialect. He was a quick study. Giovanni De Sabato, who tutored him in *solfeggio* every Wednesday and Saturday, was 80 years old and had to be helped up the stairs to the piano on the second floor of the Cocozza home.

By the age of nineteen Freddie had mastered his languages and could sight-read with the best. One day a friend, Earl Denny (one of the most popular band leaders in the East who also conducted in the church), asked Freddie's parents if they would allow him to sing the "Ave Maria" at the church on Christmas morning. They agreed and as word spread, the church filled up and the crowd spilled into the streets. Freddie was upstairs with Earl and five musicians in the choir loft. When his voice lifted in the opening notes, the entire congregation turned and looked in his direction. Even the priests were spellbound. They brought Freddie and his family into their quarters and opened a bottle of wine so that everybody present could drink to the neighborhood miracle.

Freddie was now ready for voice lessons. Mary called a family conference. Through her sister Agnes, a schoolteacher, she heard about Irene Williams, who lived and taught singing in South Philadelphia. It was decided they would look up Irene Williams, but not until they had spent the summer away from the heat of the city. So the entire family moved out to Wildwood.

As they sat on the beach one day enjoying the sunshine, the conversation turned to Freddie and his career. Everybody agreed for various reasons that Freddie Cocozza was not a good name.

An elderly woman spoke up and said, "Look at your

mother's name, how beautiful it is. Maria Lanza." Nobody could fault that.

Somebody else said, "Freddie, why *not* Lanza? Why not call yourself Fred Lanza, or Al Lanza?"

Freddie didn't like that. Neither did Mary.

But the old lady hadn't finished. "Why don't you make the Maria into *Mario*, and call yourself Mario Lanza?"

Mary was ecstatic and if Freddie had any doubts, he kept them to himself to please his mother.

With summer ended and the family back in South Philadelphia, Mary called Irene Williams and set up an audition for her son. It was, as always, a family matter. Accompanying Mario to his first visit was Mary, Tony, Mary's sister Agnes, and Agnes's husband, Al.

Mrs. Williams had Mario sing the scales first to warm up his voice and then he sang "Recondita Armonia" from *Tosca*. "My God," she said, "that was marvelous. I wish all my pupils had such a natural voice. Please sing another." Mario sang one of his favorites, "Vesti la giubba" from *Pagliacci*.

When he had finished, the teacher rose and said, "Let's start at once." She cautioned everyone, however, that her tenure would be short. "With Mario's talent, all I can do is help him for one year. Then he will have to go to a more advanced teacher and coach." Actually he studied under her for eighteen months.

Not only did Irene Williams teach him, she took Lanza to Main Line Philadelphia's society homes to sing—and to search for a patron who would invest in his future. At one such event, after Mario had sung for four hours, a member of the Astor family approached. "If you ever need help financially," he said, "perhaps we can talk."

Mario thanked him, but his pride would not allow him to accept money. He said, "I'm not ready yet. I still want to study. But thank you."

If he wouldn't accept patronage, he never turned down an opportunity to sing. At Victor's Restaurant in South Philly he was often found singing along with the great opera records

8

that were a feature of the establishment which had been named after RCA Victor Records. The owner, Mr. De Stefano, always cautioned Mario not to be loud and argumentative but to save his voice for singing. Next to singing, Mario loved to argue about opera—primarily because he knew more than anyone and always won the debates. He also attended the weekly community concerts at the John Wanamaker Department Store, and never failed to sing and sop up the adulation.

It was only a matter of time before somebody who could help advance his career became aware of him. William K. Huff heard him sing one evening at Mrs. Williams's. Huff was the impresario of the Academy of Music in Philadelphia. Afterward he got up from his seat and handed Mario his card, saying, "We shall wait for the right time and the right man and then really show you off." Mario thanked him and promptly forgot the conversation.

One afternoon not long afterward, he was at the USO Canteen in the basement of the Academy of Music, helping a group of boys move a piano upstairs. Huff recognized him and said, "Hey, Lanza, would you like to sing for Koussevitzky? He's coming here tonight." Dr. Serge Koussevitzky was one of the premier maestros of his day. Would Mario like to sing for him? He certainly would.

It was a very nervous young man who returned to the Academy that evening and waited in the wings until Koussevitzky was finished on stage. Nobody applauded more sincerely or longer than Mario. Later, as Dr. Koussevitzky was relaxing and having an alcohol rub, Huff took Mario into the room to which the piano had been moved and left the door open so he could be heard throughout the backstage area and dressing rooms. Mario started to sing his old favorite, "Vesti la giubba," and Koussevitzky, with towel in arm and shirt off came into the room and listened, obviously impressed.

When Mario finished, the maestro congratulated him and caught him totally by surprise by asking, "How would you like to come and study with me at the Berkshire Music Festival? I'll award you a scholarship." This was the kind of sponsorship he

9

had been waiting for. The festival at Tanglewood, Massachusetts, was world renowned and would give him the opportunity to study and work with other artists for several weeks.

In the *Opera News* of October 5, 1942, Herbert Graf, reviewing the festival, wrote: "A real find of the season was Mario Lanza." Lanza, he said, would have no difficulty one day being asked to join the Metropolitan Opera House in New York.

Inspired by her son's success at Tanglewood, Mary gave him five hundred dollars she had saved and sent him to New York, where he lived in a hotel, very much alone—and depressed. His money went fast and he was working with a teacher he didn't like. Finally he decided he didn't like what he was doing and was on the verge of chucking the whole business and returning to Philadelphia.

It was at this point that he met Maria Margelli, Ezio Pinza's secretary. Miss Margelli was a knowledgeable lady who had worked for years with nobility and opera stars all over the world. One night in Mario's small hotel apartment he treated her to an impromptu concert. No one is certain how deep their personal relationship went. But over a dinner which he wolfed down and she paid for, Margelli offered him a proposition.

"I'll pay for your lessons and feed you. You are the greatest voice I ever heard and I've heard them all."

For the first time in his life a woman other than his mother had some real control over Lanza's life. She found him a teacher, took him to agents and to New York society parties, making sure he was seen and heard by people who could help his career.

Margelli immediately booked Lanza for an afternoon concert at the New Jersey mansion of the owner of the La Rosa Spaghetti empire. Mary and Tony came up from Philadelphia to attend. It was the first time Mario's mother met his benefactress. Whatever resentment she may have felt about the relationship was forgotten in the happy reunion with her son.

If Margelli could be instrumental in furthering Freddie's career, then Mary would have to suffer the intrusion of another woman in his life. Still, she had apprehensions and cautioned him to be careful of "older women." Freddie sensed the jealousy in his mother and was more pleasantly amused than concerned. Mario was choosing wisely the people who would push him to the top.

2

The world was at war. Because of an eye injury suffered when he was a boy, Lanza didn't think there was a chance of his being drafted. He and Maria Margelli were in New York when Mary phoned from Philadelphia to tell him he had orders to report for his physical. Promising to return to New York immediately following the examination, which he was certain he would fail, he left for Philadelphia and a confrontation with the draft board.

To his surprise, and consternation, Lanza was drafted and inducted into the Army Air Force on December 29, 1942. Assigned to limited service because of his weak eye, he took basic training at Miami Beach, where he was housed in one of the elegant hotels on the oceanfront. Maria Margelli came to Miami and took an apartment to be near him until basic was finished and he was shipped out to Marfa Air Force Base, a semi-deserted, dusty camp on the Texas prairie. Margelli returned to New York.

The fun-loving Lanza, assigned to the Military Police, was unhappy. There wasn't much to do under the Texas moonlight in midwinter. The dust bothered his voice and the sound of the airplane engines hurt his ears. He chronicled his complaints in long letters to Margelli and his mother.

Then Lanza had a stroke of luck. Staff Sergeant Peter Lind Hayes (who, with his wife, Mary Healy, was a star in radio) was recruiting talent from within the service for a Frank Loesser show called *On the Beam*. One of the soldiers on Hayes's staff,

Johnny Silver, was culling through military records when he came upon Lanza's and discovered how much musical training the young soldier had had. Strings were pulled and Lanza was yanked from the Military Police (and Marfa) and brought to Sergeant Hayes for an audition. The prairie dust had so damaged his voice that he was unable to sing a note. Not to be deterred, Silver found a phonograph record of Frederick Jagel, a Metropolitan Opera tenor. He and Lanza quickly pasted Mario's name on the label and it was played for Hayes, who immediately accepted Lanza for the show.

Captain Fred Brisson (Rosalind Russell's husband), the officer in charge of the production, had never heard Lanza. An audition was arranged in Arizona. His voice now cleared up, Lanza asked, "What shall I sing?"

"Sing the aria you recorded," Hayes suggested. It was a selection from *Tosca*, and Mario, in typical Lanza style—collar open, feet spread like a fighter, and chest out—gave it everything he had. Brisson thought he was sensational. Hayes beamed. "You sound better than your record," he said.

On the Beam was a big success. One critic referred to Lanza as "the Caruso of the Air Force."

When the show closed after a national tour, Mario was invited to join the New York cast of Moss Hart's big production, *Winged Victory*. He was one of 342 men and women in the show. Many of them became (or already were) big names in the entertainment world, including Red Buttons, Karl Malden, Ray Middleton, Edmond O'Brien, and Barry Nelson. Since Lanza joined the show when it was already in production, he had to take a place in the chorus.

Moss Hart "discovered" him one afternoon during a dress rehearsal. Sitting in the orchestra, he was watching and listening to what was happening on stage. Lanza, behind the curtain, began to sing "Celeste Aida." Hart sat up instantly. When Lanza finished he said, "I had no idea such a voice was hidden in the chorus. That young man has a future in this business, if he wants it."

Edmond O'Brien encouraged Lanza and they became close friends. During the run of *Winged Victory* on Broadway they often visited O'Brien's mother in Scarsdale. While Mama cooked, Lanza sang Irish songs to her.

Enjoying himself, he managed to avoid the real war by helping support morale with his voice. He didn't have time to think about a career. It was wartime and careers were shelved for the duration. Nevertheless, when Warner Brothers Studios decided to film *Winged Victory*, Lanza went west with the rest of the cast. George Cukor, essentially a woman's director, was announced as director of the picture. The industry, as well as the cast, wondered how he would deal with a show that was military in nature—and mostly male. In the end he proved to be just as capable with soldiers as he was with glamorous actresses.

Maria Margelli was in Hollywood and she put Lanza in contact with a voice teacher, Mario Silva, head of the music department at Columbia Studios. There were the usual rounds of parties, and Private Lanza was kept busy meeting people and singing.

At a Hollywood party on October 5, 1944, he made an impression on some of Hollywood's notables. It was a farewell party for Warner Brothers' singing star, Irene Manning, who was leaving to entertain overseas. Walter Pidgeon came in just as Mario was finishing a session. On hearing Lanza's voice while still walking up the stairs, Pidgeon commented to his companion, "As much as I like operatic music, this is sure to be a boring evening if we spend it listening to phonograph records of the masters." So taken was he with Lanza's "live" performance, he stayed on until 3:30 in the morning to hear him sing again. That was not an uncommon response for people hearing Lanza for the first time. "Electrifying" was an adjective that was used again and again in describing his voice. Invited to come on a set where Frank Sinatra was making a picture, Lanza sang an aria from *Tosca*. A few days later Pidgeon ran into Sinatra, the swoon crooner of the day. "Who is this Lanza fellow?" he asked.

Sinatra grinned. "He's amazing. He's a soldier from the *Winged Victory* cast. He made *me* swoon!"

By the time *Winged Victory* was completed, every studio in town was aware of Lanza, thanks to people like Pidgeon and Sinatra—and Maria Margelli. Jack Warner, the hard-nosed production chief at Warner Brothers, knew talent when he saw or heard it. Through a friend, the Baroness Rothschild, Margelli arranged to take Warner a recording Lanza had made in New York. While Mario waited outside Warner's house in an old beat-up car he used during his off-duty hours, Margelli and Warner sat inside and listened to the recording of "Un Di all'azurro Spazio."

"Very nice, indeed," Warner said, "but why have you brought me a recording of Enrico Caruso?"

An executive from the Warner Brothers music department who was with them said, "If it is Caruso, then it is the best I ever heard him sing."

Margelli said, "Mr. Warner, that is Mario Lanza. He is a young soldier appearing in your own production of *Winged Victory*. Would you like to meet him? He's outside now."

Lanza was ushered in. Warner asked him,"Would you sing something in English for me?"

"If someone will accompany me," Lanza answered. The man from the music department sat down at the drawing room grand and accompanied Lanza as he sang "Serenade" from *The Student Prince*. Warner wouldn't let him stop. He then sang "Addio alla Madre" from *Cavalleria rusticana*.

When Lanza was finished, Jack Warner told him his was the best voice he'd ever heard. "I'd like to give you a contract," he said, "but your chest and shoulders are too big for the screen. You won't photograph well. Perhaps, however, you will visit me again and meet my wife. I'd like her to hear you sing."

Warner must have forgotten Clark Gable's big ears and the producers that turned him down before Louis B. Mayer pasted them back and made Gable one of the biggest stars of all time.

Lanza wasn't overly discouraged. One night Silva took him to a party given by the radio inventor and innovater Atwater Kent, at his Bel Air estate. Kent was one of the "in" hosts of the day and everybody who was anybody attended his parties. That night Art Rush, a representative of RCA Victor Records, was present. After hearing Lanza sing, Rush gave him his card and said, "You'll be hearing from us."

Lanza thought: sure, just like all the others—and he tucked the card away. Rush was not like the others, though. He was Nelson Eddy's manager and knew what he was talking about. Through him Lanza received an advance of $3,000 from RCA Victor for a recording contract. What made it unique was that he was signed without a formal audition before an executive panel or talent appraiser. The five-year contract with Red Seal was forwarded to Lanza and he became a recording star at RCA, where he remained throughout his career.

Once word was out that he had signed with RCA, publicity and promotion began. Hedda Hopper, Louella Parsons, every columnist went searching for background material on this "new" RCA Victor discovery.

Frank Sinatra urged his own manager, Al Levy, to place Mario under contract, offering a generous agreement in which he would not ask for any commissions until Mario was earning $100,000 a year. Although he declined the offer, Mario never forgot Sinatra's concern for his well-being and career.

Lanza had other pursuits besides a career. One of his soldier buddies Bert Hicks kept showing him the photograph of a girl he knew in Beverly Hills. Lanza couldn't understand why the guy would be pawning off such a beautiful girl. One day he asked him, "Is there something wrong with this girl? Why don't you go out with her yourself? She's a knockout." The soldier confessed that the girl was really his sister Betty and he was sure she and Lanza would hit it off.

Lanza was invited to his buddy's home to meet the sister. When they were introduced he gave her a hug and said, "I've known you for a long time." Her brother started to explain about the photograph. Lanza interrupted. "You talk too much. Just tell her what I told you. It was love at first sight!"

Love would have to wait. His commanding officer dampened any romantic plans by transferring him to Moore Field in northern California. Maria Margelli disappeared, taking a music-related job in Santa Barbara, California. Betty had supplanted her in Lanza's affections. He phoned her every day. It was a compulsion she would learn to live with, for Lanza had no conception of time and money spent on telephone calls—at any hour of the day or night. It could be a call across town or a three-hour marathon with someone halfway around the world. When he wanted to talk, he talked.

From California he was transferred to Walla Walla, Washington. Then in January 1945 he was given a medical discharge—not for the eye, but for a post-nasal drip. For Lanza the war was over and Betty was uppermost in his mind. Instead of returning to Philadelphia, where his mother had a coming-home party planned, he called her and told her he had some things to take care of in Los Angeles and would let her know from there what his plans were.

Betty had kept the Christmas tree up for him, though the tree was practically bare of needles by the time he saw it, and they celebrated a belated Christmas.

Soon, however, he knew he had to return to the East coast. There was the matter of his RCA Victor contract. They wanted him to come to New York to make a test record. The day finally came for Lanza to leave. But he was reluctant.

"No buts," he told Betty. "You might as well make up your mind. You can't travel with me if we're not married, and I'm not going without you. So we have to get married."

Both were Catholic, but Lanza couldn't wait.

"Come on, get your hat and coat." Grabbing her by the arm, he swept her out the door. "We'll have a religious ceremony later." They picked up a license, and the following day Lanza took Betty to a little shop where he purchased a wedding ring for $6.95. They were married the following day by Judge Griffin in the Beverly Hills City Hall.

Mr. and Mrs. Lanza boarded the train in Los Angeles and stopped off in Chicago, where Mario met the rest of Betty's family. Then, leaving Betty in Chicago, he proceeded on alone: he felt it best not to thrust a new bride on his mother without preparation. He hadn't had the courage to tell her. Now, instead of going home he went to New York and took an apartment with Johnny Silver, who was also out of the army. It was from New York that he called his mother. "Mom," he said, "just as soon as I'm really settled here in New York, I'll come to Philadelphia to see you."

Mary said, "No. We'll come to see you." Loaded with food, she and Tony arrived in New York. Lanza and Silver met them at Penn Station and, after a happy reunion, Mario took his parents to the apartment, a three and a half room suite in the Park Central. It seemed a little grander than what they expected but Mary told herself that maybe it wasn't extravagant since Mario and Johnny were splitting the rent.

Everything looked normal to Mary and she contentedly returned to Philadelphia, still unaware that her son was married. Sheepishly Lanza called Betty and explained what a mess he had made of things. She didn't scold. She tried to put herself in his mother's place: Her only son, married to a girl she didn't even know. A girl from that awful place, Hollywood. What was worse, a marriage that was not sanctioned by the church. Yes, she understood. But Mary had to know.

"I'm leaving for New York—tonight," she said. She arrived the following day, went directly to Lanza's hotel, and stood over him while he phoned his parents. "Ask them to come back to New York—and you can be the one to tell them you're married." Mario asked them to come to New York.

Shortly before Mary and Tony were expected at the apartment Betty put on her hat and coat. "I'm going to the movies. By the time I get back it'll all be settled. If your mother wants to cry, let her."

18

Mary's first words on entering the apartment were, "Where's Johnny?"

"He had to go somewhere, Mom."

"I see. So what's the big surprise?"

"It can wait. You just got here. You must be hungry."

Finally, minutes before Betty returned from the movies, Lanza began his story. He told his mother about his buddy and the photograph and meeting Betty in California. Then he said, ". . . and Mom, I asked her to marry me."

Mary listened silently, knowing there was something her son was trying to tell her, something he was omitting, but when the word *marry* popped out, she had heard enough. Her reaction was immediate. "Wait just a minute. I've listened to you, now you listen to me. How can you possibly think of marriage when you have a career ahead of you ? Think of the work involved just to get started. You won't have time for a wife. Also," she added, "how do you know this girl is good for you? For your career?"

"Mom," he said, "she's a very nice girl. She wants me to have a career and we're in love."

"I know about love. If it's real, she'll wait. So why not keep company and see what happens, okay?" She patted him on the cheek. Tony nodded his agreement. Lanza drew a deep breath. "The truth is, Mom, we're already married."

Mary's face went blank and her jaw sagged. Tony spoke the word in disbelief: "Married!" Mary couldn't believe it either. Finding her voice, she said, "If you're married, how come you're living with Johnny Silver? Where is this wife?"

"Oh, Johnny's getting his own place, and Betty's on her way home from the movies now, Mom. You're gonna just love her."

It is doubtful that Mary ever *loved* Betty. She learned to like and accept her, but her love was reserved for Mario. Under the circumstances, the first meeting of mother-in-law and daughter-in-law was as friendly as could be expected. Everybody hugged and kissed and cried; then the four of them went to St. Patrick's Cathedral to pray.

Lanza was unemployed. He had recorded "Vesti la giubba" as his test record for RCA and they said they would notify him when they were ready to make another move. In the meantime the apartment became a home away from home for many of his out-of-work singer friends. Betty accepted her husband's impractical generosity until she realized the money was running out. One morning she announced, "Mario, your friends are going to have to reduce their standard of living, and in order to help them do that we're moving into a one-room place."

Lanza said lightly, "We'll move to a bigger apartment. Remember, I was born under a lucky star."

That night the two of them went to hear his friend from the Metropolitan, Robert Weede, do a radio broadcast. After the show Lanza introduced his new bride.

"Where are you kids living?" Weede asked.

Lanza told him and added, "We're moving tomorrow—if we can find a bigger apartment."

"Wait," Weede said. "I'm living up at Nyack on my farm. Why don't you take my apartment? Nobody will be staying there."

Weede's apartment consisted of four beautifully furnished rooms on the fourth floor overlooking the skating rink at Rockefeller Center. Lanza's lucky star had come through again.

Now that they didn't have to worry about paying the rent, it was time to get down to business. First, Mario needed a voice teacher. He was brought to the attention of Enrico Rosati, who had taught Beniamino Gigli. Rosati listened as Lanza sang for him. Finally he said, "I've been waiting for you for 34 years. But I must tell you something. No one can actually teach you to sing. You had the greatest teacher of them all. God was your teacher! But come, we will work together."

Lanza and Betty were happy. No newlyweds could have asked for a nicer beginning. This was their real honeymoon. One night as they lay in bed he said, "We ought to be married in a church. It would make Mom and Pop happy." Betty agreed, and on a rainy July afternoon in New York they took the vows in a tiny chapel of St. Columbo Church, before their family and friends.

Following a year of dedicated work with Rosati, Lanza was ready. He signed with an agent, Columbia Concerts of New York, who planned an introductory tour with a warm-up concert in Toronto. Mario sang his heart out, although he was suffering from a terrible cold. During intermission he told Betty, "I should be singing the *Pagliacci* prologue. I'm more baritone than tenor tonight."

His repertoire ran from opera to the popular "Softly, As in a Morning Sunrise," an indication of his great versatility. His boyish charm captivated the crowd. Especially the women.

Betty accompanied him on tour. From the moment he opened his mouth to sing, she knew everything would be all right. The nervousness that had plagued him before he learned how to control and use his voice had gone. Twenty-five thousand people had listened to him in the open air concert at Grant Park in Chicago. Claudia Cassidy, critic for the *Chicago Sunday Tribune*, was full of praise for "Mario Lanza, a tenor, just out of the Air Forces, who, if he keeps on like this, may soon be filling the stratospheric regions of the Opera House." Emphatically Cassidy concluded: "A great new star has been born."

The following night 125,000 packed every seat to hear Lanza. It was the same throughout the tour.

3

The time had come for someone to handle Lanza's business. Sam Weiler, a small dark-haired man who sported a mustache, filled the bill. Weiler's early ambition had been to be a singer but he had given it up to become a successful real estate dealer.

Polly Robertson, a singing coach, brought Lanza and Weiler together. At lunch, they discussed Mario's freedom with money, his debts, and what they would need to start and sustain a career. Weiler made no quick decisions. He went to see maestro Peter Herman Adler, who had conducted for Lanza, and asked him, "What do you think? Will it be worth my time and effort to take him on. Does he have *that* kind of future?"

Adler assured him he did. He also quieted any fears Weiler might have about Lanza's temperament. "He has usually behaved wonderfully with me."

Adler told of an incident with Lanza in Atlantic City. Mario was appearing with the NBC Symphony Orchestra, which Adler was conducting. Mary and Tony had come from Philadelphia. After the performance, on their return to the hotel Tony opened up a bag he was carrying and said, "Now we can have some figs I brought from my fig tree."

Lanza stopped him. "Wait a minute, Pop. I have something better for you." He spread out $500 on the table, his earnings for the evening. It was the first time he had been able to pay back his parents for all they had given him.

Weiler laid down some rules when he took the job. Betty would receive $70 a week to live on. Weiler disposed of $10,000 in debts and assumed responsibility for Lanza's singing lessons and wardrobe. He became a part of Lanza's life. Mario called him "my second father." It was a Lanza trait to treat his associates as members of his family.

Columbia Concerts, pleased with the reports coming in from Lanza's most recent tour, wanted to get him out on the road again while he was still hot. They were in the process of forming the Bel-Canto Trio to tour the United States, Canada, and Mexico. Lanza and Frances Yeend (a soprano) were selected and Columbia Concerts was searching for a baritone. Several names were mentioned, but Lanza shook his head. It was the first sign of temperament in him, though he didn't see it that way. He saw it as loyalty to an old friend. He wanted George London, whose friendship he had made while making "Winged Victory" as a soldier in Hollywood. "George has the voice. All he needs is the chance." Lanza prevailed and London became the third member.

The Bel-Canto trio sang everywhere and was enthusiastically received, performing before tens of thousands of people. They missed no potential audience, even giving concerts on Indian reservations. Throughout the 86 concerts Lanza was always singled out by the critics. In Washington Park: "Lanza was the most impressive of all, with just the kind of a voice that is needed to get all the drama out." In Chicago: ". . . A coltish youngster with wide shoulders . . . Mr. Lanza sings for the indisputable reason that he was born to sing." In Oklahoma: "Mario Lanza, tenor, appears to be about 25, built like a fullback, and definitely on his way to the leading tenor in any opera house he sees fit to join."

Betty did not accompany Mario on the tour, so there was no restraint on his spending. Consequently the Bel-Canto Trio lived like kings. Lanza picked the best hotels, restaurants, and night clubs. The tour would have gone faster, but he insisted on taking the train, complaining that airplane engines hurt his ears. At one point they missed their connection after a night of frolicking and had to board a local bus into Mexico City, with a long series of stops in small towns along the way. The roads were bumpy and the three singers were crowded in with mothers, babies, and even livestock. It was hot and Lanza's and London's voices were parched. One of the Mexican passengers passed a bottle of wine and their voices cleared. In the next instant the two men burst into a duet and everybody forgot the heat and dust.

Word of Bel-Canto's successful tour reached Art Rush at RCA Victor in Hollywood. He was particularly pleased to learn of Lanza's standout performances and the rave reviews he was receiving. Ferruccio Tagliavini had pulled out of a concert date scheduled at the Hollywood Bowl on August 28, 1947. Rush knew the Bowl was looking for a substitute. Time was running short and they doubted that enough publicity would be generated by whomever they found. Rush went to the promoters and offered Lanza. He brought along a sheaf of press clippings and rave reviews to prove that his client would not only be a good fill-in but be better than the original singer.

The Bowl management had serious doubts about that, but with their backs to the wall they agreed to take Lanza. Lanza did not share their lack of enthusiasm, but as opening night drew near he realized ticket sales were low because of Tagliavini's cancellation. Lanza was not well-known enough to sell out a big concert on his own. Something would have to be done to prevent a disaster. Rush invited Walter Pidgeon, already a Lanza fan, and Ida Koverman, secretary to the MGM film mogul, Louis B. Mayer, to the concert. He knew Koverman's taste in music, and more important, her influence with Mayer.

Rush then flew Lanza into Los Angeles, got the entertainment editors and critics together for the dress rehearsal the day before the concert, and waited for the results. Their rave reviews appeared on the morning of the concert. By concert time the Hollywood Bowl was a sellout.

Lanza tripped over a wire coming on stage and laughed

nervously with the audience as he stood before them in his new white formal jacket. "I suppose if I fail here tonight they'll say Lanza fell on his face," he said. It was an unusually casual entrance for an operatic singer.

When the evening was over Lanza received the longest sustained applause ever for a newcomer at the Bowl; it lasted 15 minutes.

Ida Koverman told Pidgeon, "We must have this boy at Metro." The critics gave her ammunition the following day. *The Herald Examiner:* "Bowl singer wins acclaim. Lanza could have taken the bowl with him, judging from the bravos. . . ." The *Times:* ". . . Mario Lanza electrifies the audience . . . the sort of youth all the world loves." It went on and on as had the encores, ending with "E Lucevan le Stelle" from *Tosca,* which brought down the house.

On the strength of the reviews Koverman convinced her boss to see Lanza. At their first meeting Louis B. Mayer took an instant liking to him. Betty, who had come out to Los Angeles for the concert, was with her husband. They sat and held hands like two young kids as Mayer, behind his desk, began pushing the buttons and pulling the strings that would bring about Lanza's audition at MGM.

One of MGM's largest sound stages was set up with chairs and the hierarchy of the studio were called in, including producers, writers, and musicians. Mayer, who seldom interfered in auditions, stepped forward on the empty stage and said, "I want all of you to hear a voice." From the loudspeakers came Lanza's voice, singing the aria "Che gelida manina" from *La Bohème.*

Producer Joe Pasternak, who was part of the assemblage and who had made musicals with Deanna Durbin and Judy Garland, told Mayer, "The voice sounds like Caruso coming back to life. Who is it?"

Mayer waited until another aria was sung from the test set and then, thanking his employees for taking the time to listen (as if they had a choice), he said, "Now I want you to meet the young man who is the owner of such a God-given voice."

Lanza emerged from the set, smiling and slightly embarrassed. The film people loved him. Mayer waved his hands. "There is more," he said. "I plan to sign this young man to a term contract. I wanted you to all hear and see him. If any of you have any ideas for a film centered around him, please bring it to my attention."

The following day Mario and Betty were invited to lunch with Pasternak at the MGM Commissary to discuss his future. Lanza, excited by all that was happening to him, brought his parents out from Philadelphia to share in his success, and the night following the lunch with Pasternak, he, Mary, and Betty were guests of Pasternak and his wife in their Beverly Hills home.

Shortly after his initial meeting with Mayer, the studio head signed Lanza to a seven-year contract. He was given a $10,000 advance on signing and a starting salary of $750 a week for twenty weeks. The contract bound him to MGM for six months of the year. The other six he could devote to concerts, opera, studio and radio or other personal appearances. Lanza would receive $25,000 for his first picture, which had not yet been decided on. His second film would pay him an additional $50,000 and following films would bring his earnings to $100,000 a picture.

"Sam," Lanza told his manager, "you're not getting ten percent anymore. I'm raising your commission to twenty percent." He patted Weiler on the head and said in perfect Yiddish, *"A laben in dein kepula,"* which means, "a loving on your head."

4

Pasternak found a project for Lanza and asked him to come back to the West Coast to take care of some pre-production matters. There was also the problem of finding a place to live in California. Lanza informed Pasternak that his wife was pregnant and would have to take it easy. Joe laughed. "That's nothing. My wife is pregnant, too, and so is Kathryn Grayson, who will be your co-star in the picture."

Arriving in Los Angeles, the Lanzas rented a small house in the San Fernando Valley and Mario purchased a 1946 Oldsmobile to get him back and forth to MGM Studios in Culver City. At 200 pounds, he was overweight, and for the first time in his life that meant something. He was too heavy for the cameras—especially with his big chest and wide shoulders, which made him appear even heavier than he was.

Kathryn Grayson's pregnancy would give him a chance to get into shape. The picture, *That Midnight Kiss*, couldn't start until after the birth of her child. MGM sponsored a *Night at the Hollywood Bowl* with Lanza and Grayson appearing in concert. Miklos Rózsa conducted for them, and André Previn, then about 18 years old, also appeared on the program. Once again the Bowl audience thundered with bravos for Lanza.

He also learned about "benefit performances" at this time. Ida Mayer Cummings, Louis B. Mayer's sister, was involved with many charitable functions and the entire stable of MGM stars was somewhat at her disposal. Lanza was no exception. He found himself one day performing at a Pickfair garden party, the proceeds of which went to The Jewish Home for the Aged, Mrs. Cummings's favorite community project. It was at this event he met Giacomo Spadoni, a music coach, who had been a confidant of Enrico Caruso. Spadoni, a tall, graying, elegantly dressed man in his sixties, was on staff at MGM. Lanza embraced Spadoni and told him they must work together. "I have to sing for you. We must train for the film. When can we start?"

Spadoni, pleased and amused by the younger singer, said, "Come with me now. We'll go over to my office and run through some music."

Before the day was over the two Italians had gone through several arias, cried together, hugged each other numerous times, and promised to have their families get together.

"I like you, Maestro. You will always be with me. One day you must meet my father and mother—and Mom is a great Italian cook." Lanza meant every word he said, and another member was added to his "family."

It was around this time that Terry Robinson, a young physical fitness expert, arrived in Hollywood. One day he was called on to treat Louis B. Mayer, who was suffering from a bad back ailment. Mayer was impressed with Terry, a former amateur boxing champion and Mr. New York City. He told him about a new young singer the studio had signed. "This boy," he said, "could be a very big star but he needs to lose weight for his first picture. Maybe I could interest him in coming to you."

Not long afterward Terry was working out at a local gymnasium when a dark-haired, handsome young man in a brown suede jacket came up to him. His belt was cinched tightly but it didn't conceal his weight problem. "Are you Terry Robinson?" Terry nodded. "I'm glad to see you," he said, thrusting out his hand.

"Do I know you?" Terry asked.

"My boss is Louis B. Mayer and he thinks you can help me lose twenty pounds. My name is Mario Lanza. I have to get in shape for a picture and I'm also looking for a place to live in Beverly Hills because my wife is pregnant."

Terry asked Lanza to come to his apartment in Westwood to discuss the matter. "Once we have you started, I'll help you find a place to live."

Next morning Betty and Mario struggled up the hill in their used car to Terry's apartment. Lanza was fascinated with Terry's television set, a luxury he didn't possess yet. Terry worked out an exercise program for him. "Get yourself a sweat suit, have your wife put you on a sensible diet, and we'll start right away. I intend to reduce your weight while strengthening and toning your body."

"You see, Betty," Lanza said, "didn't I tell you he would take care of me? Okay, let's go to lunch." Mario, irrepressible as ever, was thinking of his stomach first.

At the Brown Derby in Hollywood he ordered a giant tuna fish salad and saluted their new "partnership." He and Betty cuddled like honeymooners.

It was the end of November. Betty was in her eighth month of pregnancy and it was chilly outside. She bundled up in Terry's convertible and they all went house-hunting in Beverly Hills. They found a duplex apartment on Spalding Drive, near Beverly Hills High School.

The following day they moved from the Valley to their new home. George Eiferman, then Mr. America and a friend of Terry's, helped them. They became hysterical with laughter as they wondered what the neighbors must be thinking. "We look like part of a football team," Betty said. They did: Lanza over 200 pounds, George at 210, Terry a solid 180, and Betty bulging out in all directions.

The Lanzas and Terry Robinson became friends immediately and it was not long before Mario was referring to Terry as "part of my family."

Under Terry's guidance Lanza began working out with weights and a medicine ball. Everybody was pleased, but nobody more so than Louis B. Mayer. The one thing Mayer didn't need was another overweight singer. Judy Garland was already giving him ulcers with her periodic eating binges in the middle of a picture.

Lanza went to the studio every day to familiarize himself with the script, learn the techniques of prerecording and voice dubbing, and get acquainted with wardrobe and makeup people. Wardrobe presented a minor problem. Every day he would go for fittings and every day he would be lighter. Mayer smiled. "It's easier to pad than to have a balloon on camera," he said. "Don't worry about it."

Two music coaches were assigned to the picture. Maestro Spadoni handled the operatic numbers and Irving Aaronson worked on the popular songs.

Terry was spending more and more time with Lanza. One afternoon when Mario was ready to begin prerecording his songs for the picture, he said to Terry, "You know, Terry, I hate to drive. I have to study and think of my music. Why don't you drive me to the studio?"

Terry was given no chance to object. When they got to MGM, Lanza arranged to have a studio pass issued to him and Terry sat in the recording studio and heard Mario record "Mamma mia, Che vo' sape?" Terry remembers it as the first time he really experienced Lanza's magnetism, the almost hypnotic effect he had in his personal contacts with people.

They arrived home that evening, December 8, 1948, and found Betty going into labor. The three of them got into the car and Terry drove to Cedars of Lebanon Hospital. The doctor told them the baby probably wouldn't arrive until next morning and suggested the men go home. Lanza kissed his wife and promised that Terry would stay with him so she wouldn't worry. In the morning he phoned the hospital and nothing had happened yet, so he and Terry went to the studio. Lanza was in the middle of recording "Celeste Aida" when a call came from the hospital. Terry held the line until the song was over. "Here, Mario, it's for you."

Lanza took the phone. In a moment he broke into a grin

and yelled, "Hey, I'm a father! It's a girl!" The crew gathered around and congratulated him. Pasternak, sensing it was useless to try to work for a while, said, "Mario, get out of here. Go on over to the hospital and be with your wife and daughter."

This time the new addition to Lanza's growing family was a real member: Colleen.

The recordings had been done in one take. Joe Pasternak and Louis B. Mayer envisioned the possibility of a new romantic pairing on screen. Lanza and Kathryn Grayson were being compared to Nelson Eddy and Jeanette MacDonald.

When shooting began on the picture, Terry had Lanza down to a trim 180 pounds. Studio publicity people picked up the piano-moving incident which had led to Lanza's introduction to Serge Koussevitzky. Pasternak incorporated it into the film. Lanza's role was that of an ex-GI truck driver from Philadelphia who moves a piano and becomes an opera singer. The publicity department built a campaign around the myth that he had once been a truck driver.

Lanza's first screen test for the picture was a disaster. His broad chest looked out of proportion on the screen, and the cut of his clothes had to be altered to disguise it. His hair appeared kinky and had to be straightened somewhat and combed differently. Joe Pasternak was a patient man with an eye for detail. The second tests were successful and even the still photos were better than had been expected. Some of the old-timers around the studio thought Lanza looked like a young Valentino; others saw in him a "singing Gene Kelly."

Lanza was a fast learner. Norman Taurog directed the picture, and MGM surrounded Kathryn Grayson and Mario with the best supporting cast possible: Jose Iturbi, Ethel Barrymore, Keenan Wynn, J. Carrol Naish, Jules Munshin, Thomas Gomez, Marjorie Reynolds, and Arthur Treacher. Lanza learned from all these veterans and appreciated their help. He also received advice from unexpected quarters. The

31

grips, sound technicians, electricians, just about all the crafts people had an idea how he could do a scene better or say his lines differently. All of this advice confused him, and one day he spoke to Keenan Wynn about it.

"My boy," Wynn said, "you see that man over there?" He pointed to Norman Taurog, who was busy discussing angles with a cameraman.

Mario nodded.

"That is the *only* person you listen to. Your director. He is responsible for the outcome of this picture and he will not tell you anything wrong. You do just as he says and you'll have nothing to worry about."

Lanza frequently recalled it as the soundest advice on movie acting that he would ever receive.

Movie-making, he found, was difficult work. He was required to arrive at the studio at 6:00 A.M. for makeup, then go to wardrobe, then go over the script on the set with the director and cameraman and other actors. There was a lot of sitting around and waiting for shot setups and sound tests. Lights had to be refocused several times for different angles.

Lanza had Terry bring his weights on the set, and that led to minor hassles with the makeup and hairdressing people. At any moment Lanza might decide to work out and his makeup and hair would have to be redone.

During the shooting of the picture he became good friends with Irving Aaronson, his voice coordinator, and with Ray Sinatra of the MGM music department. It was not unusual for him on the spur of the moment to invite Irving, Ray, and their wives to his apartment to listen to records and dine.

Although Lanza came home tired from the studio, he always went over the entire day's activities with Betty as he held Colleen in his arms and rocked her to sleep. "My mother," he would say, "did this to me every night. Mom always sang me to sleep." Then he would sing a lullaby for his baby daughter. It was the most tender part of the day for him, his way of unwinding.

Colleen was baptized in St. Paul's Church in Westwood.

Mario and Betty got special permission for Sam and Selma Weiler, both Jewish, to be godparents for their daughter.

With stars like Clark Gable, Jimmy Stewart, Robert Taylor, Van Johnson, Lana Turner, June Allyson, Mickey Rooney, Elizabeth Taylor, and Judy Garland on the lot, very few people paid attention to Lanza off the set. He was a greenhorn in the big film factory. Even the studio workers only nodded, and Lanza was not hounded by fans at the studio gates as the other stars were.

The picture was completed on time and previewed without advance notice in a theatre in Westwood Village on August 25, 1949. Mario, Betty, and Terry sat in the back row and Lanza was like a little boy enjoying the movie and the thrill of the audience applauding after each of his songs. MGM officials were delighted and not a little bit surprised when every preview card spoke in glowing terms of Mario Lanza, the star to be.

Lanza had to fly to New York to record his first album for RCA Victor. The recording company had everything set up for him, including a selection of three conductors. He turned them all down. "I have someone else in mind," he said to Manny Sachs, head of RCA record production. It was useless to argue with Lanza once he made up his mind, so his friend Constantine Callinicos (a young conductor he had met through Columbia Concerts before his first tour) got the assignment.

Lanza decided it would be a nice gesture to have Mary and Tony come to New York for the recording session, but when he called them Tony told him that Mary was in the hospital. It was an old problem that she had neglected for many years and now she would have to have a kidney removed, a serious operation. Lanza was getting ready to record but he was worried. Mary always came first with him, above everybody— including Betty.

He recorded some of the songs for the album and while technicalities were being worked out on the other arrangements he and Costa (his nickname for Callinicos) rented a car and drove from New York to Philadelphia. The operation had not been performed. Mary couldn't face it.

"The kidney must come out," the doctor told him, "or your mother will die. There is no middle ground."

Lanza begged his mother to go through with the operation. "I'll be near you, Mom. I'll go back to New York, finish the album, and rush right back."

She finally gave in. "All right. My Freddie is here. I'm not afraid anymore. Go ahead and do your crazy operation."

The recording sessions went quickly. One song, "Che gelida manina," from *La Bohème* is now in the RCA Victor "Hall of Fame." Other songs in the album were "Celeste Aida," "Mamma mia, che vo' sape?," "Core 'ngrato," "They Didn't Believe Me," and "I Know, I Know, I Know."

As soon as the last note was sung, Lanza and Costa were off to Philadelphia. At Jefferson Hospital Lanza arrived as Mary was getting ready to go into surgery; they were waiting for her son's return. The operation was a success, and as Lanza left to go on tour, he told the doctor, "Spare no expense. I want my mother to have only the best."

The tour was an unhappy experience for him. He missed his wife and baby and he didn't have Terry with him. He used the telephone constantly, first to Philadelphia and then to Hollywood, and made up his mind that never again would his family be so split up. Mary and Tony would have to move to California.

5

The world was about to get Lanza fever, and Lanza's life would never be the same. Encouraged by the preview responses to *That Midnight Kiss*, MGM sensed it had something unique in its new star. Lanza would become "a singing Clark Gable," Louis B. Mayer said. Joe Pasternak's view was more down-to-earth but no less enthusiastic. "This is the first time I can safely let an opera tenor sing," he said, "without praying that the audience will close its eyes and visualize Van Johnson instead."

The first major national publicity for Lanza came in the September 3, 1949, issue of *Colliers Magazine*: a new Caruso would soon appear on the silver screen. More interviews followed, one feature writer asking Lanza what would become an increasingly sensitive question: "You have been quoted as saying that you are more anxious to sing at the Met than anything else in the world. Why don't you?"

Lanza answered, "I'm not experienced enough for the Met. Caruso didn't come into his own until he was 33. At 27 I'd be rushing it."

MGM planned a national tour for Lanza and Kathryn Grayson. RCA Victor would release the first Lanza album exclusively in the cities where the film was to open. The train left Los Angeles with an entourage including Lanza and Betty; Grayson and her husband, singer Johnny Johnston; Maestro and Helen Spadoni, and Lanza's mother and father. Terry stayed behind to look after Colleen.

The pace of the tour was frenetic. Bulletins went out to the theatres alerting them to the two stars' publicity appearances. Disc jockeys were furnished two 12-inch unbreakable records in a special envelope with a picture of Lanza on the cover and a biography inside. On September 29 MGM sponsored a half-hour coast-to-coast NBC radio special featuring Lanza and Grayson.

When the troupe arrived in Philadelphia, Lanza was welcomed as a home-town hero. Streets were decorated in his honor and a procession, led by the mayor, made its way to the house where he was born.

His old neighborhood friends threw a big party. The crowd outside the house numbered in the thousands, and people chanted, "Mario! Mario!"

Johnny Johnston tried to calm them down by going to the window with his guitar and singing. They drowned him out. They wanted Lanza. It was only after he appeared at the window to a tumultuous roar that they quieted down.

Lanza was hungry but there were too many people in the house and no room to eat, so the party decided to go in search of a restaurant.

The police escort was hard-pressed to contain the hysteria both inside and outside when it learned Lanza was leaving. Escorted by uniformed officers he made his way down the stairs from the second floor and was attacked by fans who tore his shirt collar, ripped buttons from his suit, and even tried to pull the hair from his head.

Lanza and Betty were shoved into a police car and rushed out of the neighborhood. Only after he and his wife were safe in their Ritz-Carlton suite did the full impact hit him. He fixed himself a huge drink to calm his nerves.

Nursing a slight hangover the morning after, he told Betty, "It's a miracle no one was hurt. I never want to face a mob like that again!" But he would—many times.

That Midnight Kiss assured Lanza a successful future in films. It also took away all rights to any privacy he had. His face was recognized wherever he went and the clamor was always "Sing, Mario, Sing." He once complained to Terry, "You have a name. People call you Terry. I have no name. My name is 'Sing.' "

His records were selling faster than RCA Red Seal could ship them. The *Hollywood Reporter* itemed: "The Mario Lanza Album is the biggest Red Seal seller in years." *Time* magazine described Lanza as a young tenor with "the spry nonsensical air of a chipmunk."

The media hailed Lanza as a "new discovery," something MGM did not discourage. Louis B. Mayer believed that the American public loved anything "new." Fan mail poured into the mail room at MGM. On his return from the tour Lanza found stacks of personal mail, so much that the studio couldn't handle it all. They just didn't have enough people to take care of the growing volume—and were reluctant to put on extra help in the mail room.

Joe Pasternak was already arranging a new film to co-star Lanza and Kathryn Grayson. Originally titled *The Kiss of Fire*, it was later changed to *The Toast of New Orleans*. RCA was setting up new recording dates. It was important to follow a hit record or album with another as quickly as possible in order to capitalize on the public's appetite.

Ever the fun-lover, Lanza began to find whatever relaxation he could in parties. The Lanzas rented a larger house at 810 North Whittier Drive in Beverly Hills, a sprawling two-story Spanish style house with a swimming pool. The first car in the garage was Lanza's brand new Cadillac, a traditional status symbol for a movie star in the late Forties.

Mary and Tony arrived from Philadelphia with a check for $7,200, representing the proceeds from the sale of their home and furnishings. Mary asked her son to turn the money over to Sam Weiler to invest for them; it represented their life savings.

Anxious to show Hollywood what a beautiful mother he had, Mario planned a big welcoming party for Mary. All of his new cinema friends were invited to meet her and partake of her old country Italian recipes which had been in the family for generations. "We'll show them how we give a party in South Philly, Mom," he said, giving her a big hug.

Although she worked all day preparing many of the authentic dishes her son loved, it was to be a big disappointment for everyone.

The drinking started early and most of the guests never touched the elaborate spread of food she had prepared. Mario tried to explain to his guests just how each dish was prepared, but most of them kept drinking and had little thought of food.

At the end of the evening Mario and his family surveyed the party's wake: cigarettes in the food, ashes all over the furniture—a cigar ground out on their carpet. He was embarrassed and halfheartedly made excuses for the rudeness of his guests. Mary and Tony had never seen such a spectacle of inconsideration. If this was Hollywood, it was indeed a strange contrast to the family atmosphere of South Philadelphia.

Nonetheless, the Lanza home became a mecca for actors, musicians, and hangers-on. Laughter and song filled the house nightly. Nick Brodszky, a songwriter of Hungarian descent, was a frequent guest. MGM had signed him to do the score for *The Toast of New Orleans*.

In order to make his new star feel comfortable and a part of the MGM "family," Louis B. Mayer invited Mario to his home for dinner. Terry accompanied him. Over an after-dinner drink, Mayer confided his star theories to Mario. "Mario," he said, "I'll tell you what makes a star. When every woman in the theatre, regardless of age, wants you for herself, and every man want to be you—then you will be a star."

Mario listened respectfully. "I'll tell you something else," Mayer added. "The public buys you and you're a winner. The minute they turn their backs on you, you lose. So please them, Mario. Always please them."

"Mr. Mayer," Lanza responded, "God put this voice in me. Millions of people will now sit in theatres and hear opera on the screen. I'm a very lucky fellow and I thank you."

Mayer nodded. "All well and good, son, but don't forget what I said. You must *always* please the public. The public comes first."

Wherever he went, Lanza was recognized. Women would drive up alongside him on Sunset Boulevard and scream, "Mario! Mario!" They often ignored Betty or gave her only contemptuous glares. At the gates of the studio fans lined up for his autograph. Lanza couldn't wait to get home every night and have a couple of drinks to relax before the party, whether it be at his place or somebody else's.

He was keeping in condition in spite of the parties and his increasing drinking. Every morning after a light breakfast, he and Terry worked out in a small gymnasium Lanza had built near the pool. It was a rigorous routine.

Terry was now spending ten hours a day with him. His nonphysical duties also increased. Lanza needed help with his daily appointments, and Terry kept many of them for him. They were putting together a music room and Terry catalogued his library of music.

The Lanzas were swamped with invitations to the mansions of Bel Air and Beverly Hills, monuments to the wealth and status of the industry's top producers and creative people. Lanza was always asked to sing. At one Saturday night bash, his voice strained almost to hoarseness, he was approached by a fading singing star of years gone by who gave him some advice. "My dear boy," the man said, "tell them you have red throat. It works every time. If you don't do something to save your voice for work, you may wake up one morning and find that you no longer have a career—just wore it out too soon."

Lanza began to rely on the "red throat" gimmick to avoid becoming an unpaid entertainer at parties. The demands made on him now that he was an overnight sensation were often rude and sometimes outrageous. One day Charley Morrison, who owned the popular Sunset Strip nightclub, Mocambo, phoned Lanza. Business was off; would Mario mind if Morrison planted an item in one of the gossip columns that he was a frequent visitor to the club?

Lanza said, "Sure Charley. Anything I can do to help, just let me know."

A week or so later Betty said to her husband, "I've been reading how we're always at Mocambo; why don't you arrange for us to have dinner there tonight?"

Lanza thought it was a good idea. "I'll have Terry call and make reservations."

Morrison was delighted and promised a nice quiet table where Lanza wouldn't be bothered. Somehow word got around. When Mario, Betty, and Terry arrived, the place was jammed and they were escorted to a not-so-secluded table. Customers wouldn't leave them alone; they kept stopping by to say hello or ask for an autograph. Lanza wanted to relax and enjoy a night out with his wife.

Unexpectedly Charley Morrison went to the bandstand, took the microphone, and made an announcement: "Friends, the newest singing discovery, the Caruso of the movies, is going to sing for us—*Mario Lanza!*"

Lanza's jaw dropped. He didn't have a chance to resist. Pushed up on the small stage with no rehearsal, he improvised, picking simple songs—"O sole mio" and "Granada." After the first song, he tried to beg off but the crowd wouldn't let him. After the second song, however, Betty took matters into her own hands. "Come on, Terry, let's get him out of here," she said, and the two of them hustled Lanza out of the club.

Lanza knew he owed something to his public and when he was in the right mood he was eager to perform on or off the screen. But he felt he had been taken advantage of at Mocambo by someone he considered a friend.

The three of them finished their evening at Will Wright's Ice Cream Parlor in Beverly Hills where Mario related his disappointment of the night to a young actor friend from New Jersey, Nick Adams, who was working as a waiter to survive in Hollywood.

Adams, somewhat awed by Mario's stardom, grinned as he took their order and said, "Mr. Lanza, I'd trade places with you any day of the week."

6

Lanza described his fan mail as, "So hot I need asbestos gloves to open the letters, especially those with the full-length nudes." The nudes came from a broad spectrum of American females, bobby-soxers to grandmothers, who wanted to give themselves to him, body and soul. Young girls wrote that they were coming to Los Angeles, threatening to kill themselves if Lanza didn't meet them at the train or bus depot. Personal appearance tours began to make him nervous. He asked his friend, Frank Sinatra, how he handled the mobs who attacked him at the height of his early career. Sinatra advised wearing protective pads under his clothes. After a blonde in Philadelphia nearly pinched pieces of flesh from Lanza (two policemen were needed to pull her off), he took the advice.

Along with the love notes came the demands for money and the insulting letters that followed when the money wasn't forthcoming. He was criticized for comparing himself to Caruso (which he never did), accused of having no voice and being a product of studio engineers. It so disturbed Lanza that he stationed lights all around his house and kept them on 24 hours a day. He became obsessed with the idea that some kook would break in and harm his wife and baby.

Hundreds of tourists came to his gate and asked over the intercom for Lanza to come out and have a picture taken with them. Often they would become insistent. A typical visitor told the gardener, "I'm Mrs. so-and-so from somewhere. I saw

Mario in *That Midnight Kiss.* I help pay his salary so you better tell him to come out here and talk to me."

Well-dressed men were seen in the alley back of his home rummaging through the garbage cans for souvenirs, and as his career went into orbit he became the victim of scandal magazines and tabloids. Tradesmen and repairmen, even policemen, were paid large sums of money to pick up "inside stories" which more often than not were malicious and false gossip.

Not that Lanza didn't often crave attention. Riding in an open convertible, he would throw back his head and sing. He sang at the studio while going over his lines, in his music room above the coffee shop on the MGM lot, and while sunning by the family pool. He could be heard all the way to Sunset Boulevard, singing in his back yard. People crowded around his front gate for a free concert.

Betty decided, for Mario's protection, that the next house they moved into would have a high wall around it and be off the beaten path.

Christmas of 1949 saw the first of the big Christmas parties that became a trademark of the Lanzas. No one had a bigger or more brightly decorated tree. Terry painted a large Santa Claus on the front window facing the street and at night it was lit up. Colored lights on the lawn spelled out "Merry Christmas." It was open house and there was a gift for everyone, including strangers who wandered in off the street.

On Christmas day, after the family returned from church, Mary prepared breakfast for everyone just as she had long ago in Philadelphia. The food was enough to feed a location unit for a week.

Because of the Lanzas' extravagance it became necessary to reshuffle the growing staff and assign more specific responsibilities. Sam Weiler continued as Mario's personal manager, Jack Keller was selected to handle public relations, and Terry remained Mario's all-around coordinator and confidant.

Weiler set up a corporation for Lanza and they called it

Marsam Enterprises, combining both their names. Mario's income would be funneled into the corporation for investments. A suite of offices was rented in the Allen-Paris Building in Beverly Hills. Always loyal to old friends, Mario and Betty brought Kathryn Reitzle out from New York to be the secretary for the new corporation. Reitzle had been their neighbor during the days they lived in Rockefeller Center and both were fond of her.

Lanza was spending far into his future earnings. The Whittier Drive home began to accumulate "things," such as antiques, oversize sofas, or anything else that took his or Betty's fancy. With Lanza things didn't have to match. He bought what he liked.

Lanza had always been gregarious and free-spending. Now that he was famous and wealthy he saw no reason not to enjoy it. All his life he had given to and fed his friends. Nightly guests at the dinner table were commonplace, as was the presence of little Colleen. Lanza wanted it that way. "If she is a child of mine, she wants to be with people."

Sundays were open house. The Lanzas thought nothing of serving a barbecue to thirty unexpected guests. To Mario, it was a catastrophe one Sunday when a throng of "friends" dropped in unannounced and there wasn't quite enough chicken cacciatore to go around *twice*! The cook shook her head and said, "This is the eatingest house I've ever seen."

It was a frantic period. However, for some unknown reason, Mary and Betty seemed to have declared a truce in the silent war that was escalating toward a hot confrontation for control of the house—and Mario.

It was time to get back to work. Prerecording of songs for Lanza's second film, *The Toast of New Orleans*, was to begin almost immediately.

The night before he was to appear in the recording studio Lanza went to a big party thrown by a prominent Hollywood director. Driving with Terry and Betty to the director's estate in the Santa Monica mountains, Lanza said, "I

43

hope they don't ask me to sing tonight. I've got to work tomorrow."

"You know they'll ask you," Terry said.

"Well I don't think I'd better. Are they inviting me just because of my voice?"

Although Lanza was not a sophisticated Hollywood veteran, he knew when he was being taken advantage of. The Hollywood crowd tended to mistake him for the uneducated truck driver from South Philadelphia that had been concocted by the MGM publicity department and he began to resent it.

He arrived at the party and mingled with the other guests. Soon the host called for quiet and made the inevitable announcement: "Ladies and gentlemen, Mario Lanza is going to sing for us."

Lanza nodded to Terry, who went to the host, whispered in his ear, and returned to Mario and Betty. The host knew Terry's position with Lanza, but annoyed, he announced, "I've been informed by Mario's *bodyguard* that Mr. Lanza has a case of red throat and will not be able to sing for us tonight."

By morning the studio was buzzing with the news. Lanza had refused to sing at so-and-so's party. Lanza was getting bigheaded and temperamental. Terry picked up bits and pieces of the story and found himself in the position of having to defend Mario's decision not to sing. He realized that Lanza had been right—it was the *voice* that had been invited.

The refusal created such a ruckus at the studio that Irving Aaronson felt compelled to bring it up. "He's an important director, Mario. For weeks he told everyone that you would be at his party and that you sang at all parties. You put him in an embarrassing position."

Lanza didn't smile, nor was he frivolous when he said, "Irving, I wouldn't call him to my house to direct a picture. I guess I'll have to stay in my own home, give my own parties, and then I won't have to save anyone's face but my own."

It was the beginning of Lanza's reputation for being difficult and temperamental. Gossip columnists had their leg men and informants reporting his every move. If he gained two pounds, it was reported as twenty. When he ordered a lot of food for friends, he was said to have eaten it all himself. If his hair was uncombed or he didn't shave for a day, it was rumored he had been out all night drunk.

The gossip began to affect his family life. Betty took her hurt out on Mario's mother. When Mary complained, Lanza would blow up, leave Betty and Mary in tears, and start to drink. One afternoon when tension was high he made an announcement. He was going to rent a place for Mary and Tony, a place they could call their own. That, he hoped, would solve the problem of two women trying to run the same household. Since neither Mary nor Tony drove, he asked Terry if he would move in with them. They found a three-bedroom house on Crescent Drive in Beverly Hills. Every day Terry spent the day at the studio with Mario, then the entire family had dinner at Mario's home, and Terry returned to Crescent Drive with Tony and Mary afterwards.

Louis B. Mayer sent a memo to department heads: Anyone discovered giving gossip items about Lanza to a columnist would be dismissed. The gossip didn't bother Mayer; its effect on Lanza was what bothered him.

The prerecordings for *The Toast of New Orleans* were sensational. Some of the songs recorded were: "The Flower Song" from *Carmen*; "O Paradiso" from *L'Africana*; "M'appari," an aria from *Martha*; the duet finale from Act I of *Madame Butterfly*, plus the Nick Brodszky score: "Boom Biddy Boom Boom," "Tina Lina," "I'll Never Love You," "The Bayou Lullaby," "The Toast of New Orleans," and "Be My Love."

It was an important film with a cast that included David Niven, J. Carrol Naish, and a host of solid supporting actors. Lanza played the role of Pepe Duval, a robust Cajun shrimp fisherman in Louisiana's Bayou country. To keep in shape he brought his weights to the studio. Kathryn Grayson sometimes joined him in his exercises, showing herself remarkably adept at lifting barbells.

Lanza became friendly with the extras on the picture. One

day several of them asked if he would ruin a late scene so the day's shooting would go into overtime and they would get extra money. Extras worked on a day-to-day basis, not on contract. Lanza obliged them and was criticized by management for being difficult.

Popular with the crew and other actors, Lanza would invite them over to his dressing room during breaks to listen to albums he played on a small record player. Usually they wanted to hear Lanza records and it wasn't long before people were saying that all Lanza wanted to do was listen to his own voice.

Instead of going to the commissary for lunch Lanza had his mother prepare dozens of sandwiches which Terry brought with him in the morning. Lanza fed everybody who came by his dressing room. Even that was misconstrued. Word came out of the commissary kitchen: "Boy, that Lanza eats like a pig. You should see the food he orders."

Lanza ignored the sniping and tried to have a good time on the set. He surrounded himself with people he liked and soon everyone in the group had a nickname. Lanza became The Tiger. Terry, who had the duty of keeping pests away, was Terry the Terror. One of the prop men, getting into the spirit of things, hung a sign on Lanza's dressing room door which, in four different languages, said: *Don't Fuck with the Tiger!*

RCA Victor was delighted with the score and sent Costa Callinicos from New York to conduct the two albums Lanza would make from the film. Callinicos, who immediately picked up the nickname of Serpent, moved in with Mary and Tony on Crescent Drive for the duration of the film and recording sessions. "Be My Love" was released as a single on RCA Victor Red Seal backed by "I'll Never Love You," conducted by Ray Sinatra. For the album Lanza had selected Callinicos to conduct the opera score and Sinatra for the popular material, this time with RCA's okay.

During the filming Lanza celebrated his 28th birthday on the set with a huge cake prepared by Sarno's Bakery in Hollywood. The press outnumbered film people and later he invited them all to his home for one of Mary's Italian dinners. The amount of work meant nothing to her. She had worked all her life for one thing or another, and almost always with her son in mind. It also gave her a chance to one-up Betty, who could not compete with her in the culinary department and didn't try.

Lanza trusted columnists, as he did everybody else, frequently to his own detriment. Before long the papers began referring to him as "the fat tenor" or "the chubby tenor." One columnist reported: "It isn't any wonder Lanza is so fat—he eats 12 eggs for breakfast." Lanza ran across that particular item one morning as he, Terry, and Betty shared breakfast.

Lanza patted Betty on the hand. "What can you do? It comes with success."

But he was obviously hurt by references to his weight problem and as usual he was in a black mood for the next few days.

While the papers were pointing out Lanza's "great battle with the bulge," RCA Victor was reporting that its coffers would eventually bulge to the tune of $100,000 in royalties for Lanza from the *That Midnight Kiss* album. He received his second $25,000 bonus from MGM for completing *The Toast of New Orleans*, and Louis B. Mayer wrote him a new contract with a large salary hike.

Lanza tried to be philosophical about the silly and sometimes unkind gossip items. "I must be getting popular," he told Terry, "if they have to make up stories just to get me in their columns."

7

Lanza was asked to give a private concert for Pope Pius XII and the College of Cardinals. He declined, giving as an excuse the fact that Caruso had been 45 when he was so honored while he, Lanza, was only 28. The truth was, he was out of shape. After finishing *The Toast of New Orleans* he fell into the overeating that he had kept in check during filming of the picture.

The problem was exacerbated by the inconsistency of the MGM front office. An operatic singer delivers a more resonant tone when he has additional weight, so the studio would allow him to balloon up during the prerecording sessions; but immediately afterwards Mayer would beg Terry, "Get his weight down. We shoot in two weeks. He looks like an oversize cow!" Lanza's metabolism was being manipulated like a Yo-Yo.

With the film in the can, Mario and Betty took their first vacation since his Hollywood career had begun—a working vacation. Leaving Colleen in Los Angeles with Terry, they booked passage to Honolulu with Callinicos and the Sam Weilers on the S.S. Lurline. Five concerts had been lined up for the trip. The first was given at McKinley Auditorium to a sell-out crowd. It was the beginning of a very successful tour. Lanza might as well have been back in Hollywood for all the rest he got. At one personal appearance he signed his name on over 1,000 record jackets, plus photos, cards, and whatever else his fans thrust at him.

The pace began to tell on Betty, who drank a little more

than she normally would have. But Lanza thrived on public acceptance and returned to Los Angeles in an exuberant mood.

Before the Hawaiian tour, he had entertained the Oriental impresario, who booked the tour, and his American wife in his home while Sam Weiler completed the itinerary with both of them. There had been a lot of food and drink. At one point Lanza decided to accommodate the impresario's wife by giving her a tour of the upstairs. He motioned for Terry to follow him, a signal he often gave which meant for Terry to stand guard so nobody would come upon him in a compromising position.

Stationed outside Lanza's bedroom door, with Betty downstairs playing hostess, Terry couldn't help but overhear the sounds of lovemaking coming from behind the closed door.

After the tour Weiler told Lanza that the impresario had cheated him on commissions. He was apologetic, saying it was too late to do anything about it.

Lanza only grinned and said, "Forget it Sam. Don't worry. He screwed me, I screwed his wife."

Though he was a family man with a second child on the way, Lanza was still the same young hell-raiser who had climbed out of his grandfather's window to go girl-chasing in Wildwood so many years before.

Not long after his return from Hawaii Lanza was invited to sing at a Friars Club function which was being given at the Los Angeles Shrine Auditorium. He shared a dressing room with violinist Isaac Stern and the unpredictable Errol Flynn. When Stern left the room to find a quiet place to practice, Flynn began to regale Lanza with bawdy stories. Both men were drinking and Flynn, who had consumed a full bottle of vodka, asked him how such a handsome guy managed to sing "so damn big and strong."

Lanza laughed. "Errol, you should be great yourself as a singer. You've got what it takes to sing." He borrowed an old Yiddish expression: "You've got to have *batzem* (balls)."

Flynn tipped his hat and inside the crown he had taped his

lines for the evening. "You don't think I'd go out there and face a live audience without a little help," he confessed, making a grab for a young actress passing by.

Lanza loved men like Flynn and they often exchanged humorous stories about the women they had taken to bed.

Lanza was a young man on the verge of success when Terry first met him. He had an appealing zest for life—eating, drinking, and being merry. Like most young men, he had an eye for attractive women. When success came he was still the friendly, cocky youngster who had grown up doted on by his mother. He didn't have time to learn the restraint that ten more years of struggle might have taught him and he wasn't prepared for the constant insecurity of being a star. With fame the behavior of both Mario and his wife grew increasingly unstable.

Betty, who always suffered during pregnancy, was becoming a tyrant around the house. She fired help for no reason and complained constantly that good help didn't exist anymore. She was taking pain-killing medicine. She was also drinking more.

Few knew just how much she was drinking at first because she was careful. It came out when one of the maids, cleaning off the dinner table, took a sip from Betty's glass of milk. She spit it out and made a face. "This is sour!" Another member of the staff tasted it and said, "This isn't sour. It's damned near 100 proof Scotch whiskey!"

They began to watch Betty closely. Rather than tell Lanza, one of the maids brought it to Terry's attention. Over several weeks he determined that Betty was spiking not only her milk but practically everything she drank. He didn't want to say anything to Lanza, who was under pressure getting ready to do another film. He mentioned it to Betty, telling her she ought to be careful because of the baby. She shrugged it off. "A drink with dinner isn't going to hurt me or the baby. Don't listen to household gossip, Terry."

Nevertheless, Betty's drinking provoked more and more

arguments with Lanza. He would invariably storm out of the house with Betty yelling after him, "That's right. Go to your mother. She'll baby you." Terry would take him either to Mary's or to the Casa D'Amor Restaurant in Hollywood which was owned by his friend Franklyn D'Amour, an old vaudevillian. Lanza was always admitted through the back door and seated at a back table out of sight from the curious.

Eventually Terry would be asked to call Sam Weiler and request his intervention with Betty. Once she was pacified, Lanza would return home. They would kiss and make up, usually all the way from the front door to the bedroom. It became a familiar pattern, and in time Terry and everyone around the Lanzas grew tired of being embroiled in the temper tantrums and childish pouting.

Although Lanza always said he never wanted to be a movie star, he began to act like one. He and Betty would stay up all night drinking and partying, and sometime in the afternoon they would have breakfast in bed. He missed rehearsals and was given a "fatherly" lecture by Louis B. Mayer. He fell to listening to gossip and believing it. Whoever was nearest had his ear.

The minute Lanza began to be famous, of course, everybody wanted something from him. Maestro Spadoni wanted more money and asked Lanza to help him stay on at MGM. Lanza's relatives in Philadelphia wanted to come out to Hollywood and be given work at MGM; his Uncle Robert, a dress designer, wanted to design for the movies.

Lanza paid for everything. He had a public relations man who also had other clients, but it was Lanza who paid the office rent and expenses. It was "the time of the leeches," as Terry said.

If his home life was shaky, life on the streets was impossible. He adopted a disguise—felt hat, glasses, fake nose—to hide his identity. The one place away from home where he felt reasonably at ease was Palm Springs. He rented a house there on a year-round lease and often left on the spur of the moment to hide out in the desert.

Lanza also had an apartment on the MGM lot that had once belonged to Frank Sinatra. He spent many nights there when he and Betty were having one of their fights that went on for weeks. They were rarely lonely nights. Usually starlets could be seen leaving the apartment in the morning, rushing to the sets where they were performing.

MGM wanted to release *The Toast of New Orleans* and take advantage of Lanza's popularity. Gene Ruggiero, who was the film editor of Lanza's pictures, screened the picture for Dore Schary, one of Mayer's top production men. Schary didn't like the film and phoned Mayer. "We have a 3 million dollar lemon on our hands," he said.

Mayer, upset, called Ruggiero and requested that a print he brought to his home so he and Mrs. Mayer could look at it and judge for themselves. When the last reel was finished and the screen went blank, Mrs. Mayer said, "Louis, I love it. It is a great picture." Mayer agreed. "What the hell is Schary talking about? What's he got against Lanza and Grayson?"

The reports on *The Toast of New Orleans* from the exhibitors were fantastic, confiming Mayer's belief. RCA Victor was readying an album for release and a single of "Be My Love," a song from the movie. Now it was important to prepare a new project for Lanza. Since he was constantly compared to Caruso, it was inevitable that somewhere along the line he would be tabbed to play the great tenor. His third film at MGM was already on the drawing boards and would be called *The Great Caruso*.

Readying himself for a new picture meant putting on pounds for the prerecordings and then slimming down for the camera, which always left him in a harried state. On top of that, Betty's behavior was getting more erratic.

One night Lanza went into the kitchen and found that his wife had boarded up the back staircase for no reason. The help complained that the house was being run like a military base and Lanza, trying to keep peace, slipped the servants extra money to keep them from quitting. Some took the money and quit anyway.

At the same time the whole world continued to act as if Lanza were public property. One night, after a performance at the Hollywood Bowl in which he gave everything he had, Mario took a party, including his wife, parents, and Terry, to Ciro's nightclub to see Dean Martin and Jerry Lewis perform. From the stage Lewis announced the names of celebrities as they entered and the ovation for Lanza went on and on. Finally, as the crowd quieted down, the comedian said, "If he's that important, let's get him to sing."

"No, no," Lanza declined. "I've just come from a concert and want to relax."

The irrepressible Lewis persisted, bringing the microphone over to the table and thrusting it in his face. "I'll stay here until you sing."

Lanza shrugged and asked Spadoni to accompany him with the old standby, "Vesti la giubba." When the wildly appreciative applause subsided, Lewis announced from the stage, "Ladies and gentlemen, the show is over. No one can follow that performance."

8

After two films with Kathryn Grayson, Lanza wasn't sure he wanted to work with a new co-star. For his next picture, *The Great Caruso*, Ann Blyth had been chosen to play opposite him. He had never met her but several of the hangers-on who seemed to delight in creating problems on the set told him she was difficult to work with. Lanza decided to worry about it later. Right now he had to deal with MGM. The studio wanted someone from their own organization to handle the musical chores for the film. Lanza, as always when it came to his conductor, had ideas of his own. He wanted Dr. Peter Herman Adler from New York.

Louis B. Mayer was against it, but Lanza didn't leave him much alternative. "If you want the best performance I can give musically, I need the conductor I know can do the best job for me." Mayer finally relented and put Adler on salary. But he warned, "Mario, my executives tell me that a movie about opera won't make much money. I'm banking on you to prove them wrong." Mayer had another reason for wanting the picture to be successful. "I'm stepping down as head of the studio and I'd like to go out on top. You've got to make this a real winner for us—for me. You think you can do that?"

Lanza assured him he could. On leaving Mayer's office he told Terry, "That man is a giant. A lot of people don't like him. I love him. He knows how to treat his actors. When he leaves the studio everybody in the business will miss him."

While *The Great Caruso* was in the pre-production stage, *Modern Screen* magazine set up an appointment to interview Lanza and a writer was sent out to the house. Terry went behind the bar and prepared a round of drinks. One round led to another and pretty soon the three of them were swapping stories. Terry told about the tough Brooklyn neighborhood he lived in until the age of 14. The writer responded with stories of the gangsters in the neighborhood he grew up in. Lanza's normal childhood seemed lost in the shuffle of Terry and the writer matching tough backgrounds. After the interview Terry phoned the writer's girlfriend and had her pick him up; he was in no condition to walk, much less drive.

When *Modern Screen* published the article, Lanza was quoted as saying that Philadelphia during his childhood was a town of gangsters and the worst city in the United States. The citizens of South Philadelphia, many of them long-time friends, were angered. Some went as far as to smash the windows in Grandpa Lanza's store and destroy Mario's records in Nick Petrella's record shop.

Lanza was hurt that his friends in South Philadelphia would believe such a story. "Can you believe it, Terry? Only a year ago these same people paid me the greastest respect a boy can get from his home town. Now, just one misquote and I'm a bastard."

The mail coming to the house in response to the article included a threat to kidnap Colleen. It so frightened Lanza and Betty that Terry was asked to move in with them. He slept on a day bed in the living room where he could observe the entrance and the stairway to the family's sleeping quarters. The police were notified. Full security precautions were put into effect. No packages were accepted or opened without notifying the bomb squad.

Lanza went through a period of not really knowing who to trust, even among his close friends. The vilification inspired by a mere fan magazine article was yet another unexpected hazard of stardom.

The situation finally improved when the *South Philadelphia American* ran a telegram from Lanza to the people of South Philly explaining what had happened. *Modern Screen* followed up with a story by Lanza entitled "My Home Town." But after that he was suspicious of magazine writers; although he couldn't avoid interviews, he seldom felt comfortable doing them unless it was with someone he had known for a long time.

The prerecording schedule for *The Great Caruso* was a heavy one; the score included excerpts from eighteen operas. The prerecordings produced some of the greatest music ever done for a motion picture.

Conductor Adler's accommodations at the Beverly Hills Hotel had been arranged by MGM, and he was unhappy there. He registered his displeasure one day to Lanza and Terry when they picked him up on their way to the studio.

"It is too much Hollywood for me," the maestro said. "I am a simple man. I like more homey surroundings."

"Don't worry about a thing," Lanza said, "you're moving in with Mom and Pop. Let's get your clothes and we'll do it now." He was checked out of the hotel in a few minutes and moved into Mary and Tony's place on Crescent Drive, where he felt right at home. The following morning he appeared in the Cocozza kitchen for breakfast wearing shoes, socks, a shirt, and underwear—no pants. Terry and the Cocozzas stared at him.

"What's the matter?" he asked.

"Dr. Adler," Mary pointed out, "You have no pants on."

"Oh, that's true," he said, relieved it was nothing more serious, "I never wear pants when I have breakfast at home. I feel like home here."

As long as he stayed with the Cocozzas he never appeared at the breakfast table with his pants on.

On the day they were to record "The Sextet" from *Lucia* Lanza invited his wife and parents to the set. Betty sat quietly as the stage was set up for the recording session. At that point in her relationship with Mary she spoke as little as possible to her mother-in-law. Mary had old-fashioned ideas about pregnancy and motherhood and never missed an opportunity to remind Betty that liquor and pills might cause her to give birth to a "mongoloid—or worse."

The singers were assembled. Dorothy Kirsten of the Metropolitan Opera Company was the only one among them whom Lanza had ever worked with. "Today I have to prove to the opera people that I can sing," Lanza said to Terry. "Tell Pop to listen. This one is for him."

Sixty musicians, the best available in California, had been hired. Adler ran through the music, the singers mounted their platforms, adjusted their microphones, set up the music, and prepared to record. At that moment Lanza entered and the others glanced his way. He pushed the microphone a good three feet from where he stood, feet spread wide apart, shoulders thrown back, head high. "All set, Maestro," he said. "Let's sing!"

Never had there been such a recording session of opera in films. When it was over, Adler and the entire orchestra stood and applauded. Nicola Moscona (a basso profundo) and Giuseppe Valdengo (a baritone) of the Metropolitan Opera— both in the film—rushed up to Lanza. "Come to the Met. We need your voice at the Met!" It was an emotional occasion. Valdengo went to the piano and started to play Italian songs. Moscona kissed Tony and said, "Pop, your son is the greatest tenor I ever sang with."

In truth, Lanza had never sung better.

The filming of *The Great Caruso* was Lanza's finest hour in motion pictures. He saw it as a chance to bring opera to the people. Richard Thorpe, the director, felt the same way and their relationship was the most satisfying Lanza ever had with a director.

Occasionally Lanza would make a suggestion. "I don't think Caruso would have used such an expression," he might say.

"Okay," Thorpe agreed. "You're the expert."

They worked well together and the picture came in ahead of schedule and under budget.

When the cast met for the first time to get copies of the script, they were asked to come a little early, all except Ann Blyth. The purpose was to explain to everybody that Miss Blyth, being a very religious young lady, would not tolerate swearing on the set. Lanza merely nodded.

The room grew silent when Blyth and her secretary arrived. Nobody knew what to say, all fearing that whatever came out would be the wrong thing. Lanza couldn't stand the tension; he knew if this was the way the picture was going to start, it would be a miserable experience for everybody.

He decided to do something. "Ann," he yelled, "we were warned not to swear around you, but honey, excuse us, especially me, if I yell once in a while. We have a big picture to make about a man who was known to yell and swear. He had balls. He was a real man who let go and sang like a son-of-a-bitch!"

There was a moment of embarrassed silence. Then Blyth went over to Lanza and gave him a big hug and a kiss.

"Mario, thank you! I get this at every studio. I hope it stops here. I'm so happy to be working with you."

The ice was broken and the others relaxed. Lanza and Blyth got along beautifully throughout the film.

Lanza loved to impersonate people, and *The Great Caruso* brought out his spirit of fun. One morning he arrived at the studio at 6:30, as usual, and went into makeup. The first thing he heard was the voice of Ezio Pinza in the next booth. Immediately he broke into a convincing imitation of Pinza singing "Some Enchanted Evening."

Pinza was startled and then laughed. "Mario, you son-of-a-bitch! Where are you?"

Joe Pasternak was a favorite target for Lanza's practical jokes. He once called a reporter and told him he was Pasternak and gave an "exclusive" story in Pasternak's Hungarian accent.

Another time he phoned the MGM commissary and, in Pasternak's voice, made a reservation and ordered lunch for six people. It was impossible for Pasternak or anybody else to get mad at Lanza for such things.

Now a big MGM star, Lanza was given an apartment dressing room in the same building with Clark Gable, Van Johnson, Robert Taylor, and Gene Kelly. Across the hall lived Lana Turner, Elizabeth Taylor, Ava Gardner, and Judy Garland. Louis B. Mayer kept the sexes on opposite sides of the hall. The apartment became a home away from home for Lanza and Terry. There were two beds as well as a shower, a kitchenette, and a study. They moved in barbells, a record player, and books.

There was a constant stream of visitors to the set and some of them invariably were invited to Lanza's apartment on the lot. One day the attractive wife of a high-ranking Naval officer asked him to show her around. "I have a family photo album you should see," he said. "My aunts and uncles. . . ."

He steered her to the apartment while Terry entertained her friends with a tour of the studio. Lanza's "album" consisted of racy pictures which had been sold to him by one of the bootblacks (also Lanza's bookie) at the studio barber shop. Among them were some classic shots of Joan Crawford from her very early days, a notorious photo of Carmen Miranda without underpants, and a nude shot of Joan Blondell which had been sneaked as she sunbathed on the beach.

The Naval officer's wife was entertained for several hours and when Lanza returned to the set he winked at Terry.

One scene in the picture was with an older singer, a woman who had hurt Lanza early in his career in New York. "Terry," he said, "I have to grab this woman and throw her to the floor as I sing. You'd better tell the prop men to put heavy covering on the floor, because I've never forgiven her for costing me a job in radio when I needed work."

Fortunately Terry took him at his word. In the scene, Lanza grabbed the woman and slammed her to the floor. A few days later, while walking across the lot, he heard a voice behind him crying "Mario! Mario!" It was the opera singer hurrying toward him.

"Oh, my God," he said to Terry, "she's probably going to let me have it."

Instead, she hugged and kissed him. "Mario, what a wonderful scene. So real. Thank you! Thank you! Everyone is talking about it."

Unfortunately the scene ended up on the cutting room floor.

Rita Moreno, with whom Mario had become friendly and had encouraged on *The Toast of New Orleans*, came to see him on the set of *The Great Caruso*. She had made another film and was dropped by Metro. She asked Mario if he would talk to the studio bosses. Maybe they would reconsider. She was in tears. "Look," he said, "I'll talk to Pasternak and Schary and see what I can do. Don't worry." He did try, but unsuccessfully. Dore Schary told him to mind his own business.

Mario returned to his dressing room in a fury. "Can you believe it," he stormed (while Terry listened). "They keep nobodys on big salaries and let talented kids like Rita go." He always stood by friends and in this case Miss Moreno has more than justified his faith in her talent.

One night after watching the rushes Lanza said to Terry, "We don't work tomorrow. I've been on the go, so tonight we relax. After Betty goes to sleep we'll go out and have a few beers."

At the Casa D'Amor they began to unwind over a pizza which was prepared especially for Lanza. (It eventually became a part of the regular menu as "The Mario Lanza Special.") They had both been up since 5:30 in the morning and it was now past midnight. Terry thought they ought to go home and get some sleep.

Enroute, driving west on Sunset Strip, they approached the Players, a restaurant which was popular with stars. Lanza said, "Stop here, Terry. That pizza made me thirsty. Let's have a nightcap." Inside the bar, as he and Terry sat having a beer, two men and a woman came in, already in their cups. The bartender bragged that Mario Lanza was sitting in the corner. The woman staggered over to Lanza's table and asked for an autograph. Lanza wrote: "May I wish you the very best of everything in life. Always, Mario Lanza."

One of the men took offense when she lingered at the table and he came to retrieve her. "Hey, what's goin' on here? Just 'cause you're a movie star you think you can make my girl?"

Terry tried to intercede. "He's only signing an autograph."

Ignoring Terry, the guy pushed Lanza's arm across the table and grabbed the piece of paper. Lanza, quick-tempered as always, threw a punch which sent the man sprawling. Terry quickly got him out before any press wandered into the club.

Lanza lost a shoe in his haste to get to the car, which the attendant already had waiting with the motor running. Terry took him to Vic Damone's apartment, which was nearby. He then returned for the shoe and was told by the parking lot attendant that the fellow who had been punched was minus two front teeth.

There was no bad publicity and Lanza, through Jack Keller, arranged to pay for the fellow's dental work.

The Great Caruso album, which would be Lanza's most successful and the only operatic album ever to sell a million copies, was one that he truly trained for. During the day he and Terry prepared for the evening recordings with intensive workouts by the pool. Lanza, feeling strong as a bull, lifted weights for about an hour, then had a rubdown and went to bed. Before the recording he ate a large, very rare steak, sucking the blood from the almost raw meat. He ended his meal with a glass of wine and was off to the studio. He sang four arias a night and finished the album in two nights.

Columbia Concerts was busy lining up a tour to coincide with the release of the film and the album.

Lanza had become a big business—too big for Sam Weiler to handle on his own. He urged him to sign with Music Corporation of America. Lanza often complained to Terry: "I'm a human being, not a corporation. Why can't I just sing and not have to worry about all this bullshit. Sometimes I wish I could go back to South Philly and spend my summers in Jersey with Grandpa."

On December 3, 1950, Betty gave birth to their second child, another daughter, Ellisa, named after Lanza's grandmother. Andy and Della Russell were the baby's godparents. Andy, one of the most popular ballad singers during the Forties, had become one of Mario's earliest friends in Hollywood. Mario had somewhat of a crush on Della, but kept it to himself except when he drank and poured his heart out to Terry. If Andy was aware of it, he ignored it as a one sided flame.

Lanza's career was at its peak. The old show business adage "There's no place to go but down" should have been tacked over his dressing room door as a warning.

9

Sam Weiler took care of business with Mario's power of attorney. All Mario had to think about was entertaining the public, taking care of his voice, and keeping up his health. That was the advice he constantly received.

About the same time *The Great Caruso* was completed, *The Toast of New Orleans* was released to the public. Mario was touted as not only a singer, but a budding comedian. He was not at all pleased with that. He didn't fancy himself a singing comedian and let the MGM front office know how he felt. He sent the studio executive an ultimatum: "Give me a serious dramatic picture."

Nonetheless, *The Toast of New Orleans* broke house records in theatres all over the country and in Europe as well.

In terms of career Lanza was the most secure person in Hollywood. Offers poured in from around the world. Movie magazines with his picture on the cover were guaranteed to sell out, and not a day went by that his name didn't appear in the newspapers.

When Kathryn Grayson and Johnny Johnston's divorce hit the front pages, the New York *Journal American's* Cholly Knickerbocker wrote: "Friends of Kathryn Grayson and Johnny Johnston say the divorce plans came as a complete surprise to him, but they insist there is a romance brewing between Miss Grayson and Mario Lanza, Metro's new Caruso."

Nothing could have been further from the truth. Grayson

never considered Lanza more than an overgrown boy with a golden voice.

Vice-President Alben Barkley phoned Mario personally to ask him if he would sing for President Truman at a party he was giving in Blair House on December 14. Among the numbers requested were "Be My Love" and "Vesti la giubba," which Mr. Truman had heard him sing on Hedda Hopper's radio show a few weeks earlier. Hedda reported that "Be My Love" sold 70,000 copies as a single the week following his appearance on her show.

Lanza's growing popularity unfortunately didn't extend to his home. To escape Betty's tirades he drank too much and then would gorge himself to the point of physical pain. Their arguments became more vicious. One night in a rage Mario screamed, "You were Rosie the riveter when I met you—you are still Rosie the riveter. You belong in a defense plant, not in a Beverly Hills mansion." They stopped going out together. Once again Betty took her problems, bottle, and pills to the bedroom and locked the rest of the world out.

To get away from the war at home, the following afternoon Mario took Terry by the arm and said, "Let's go for a drive. I want to think." That meant driving over to Beverly Hills, parking the car and window-shopping. Lanza loved to window-shop and one of his favorite places was The Patio Shop on Beverly Drive. It was owned by an artist friend Harry Lachmann. Two white lovebirds were caged at the shop's entrance and shoppers were sometimes surprised to come upon Mario talking with the two caged birds. During the outing he did a lot of thinking about his problems at home. He didn't enjoy sparring with Betty. But he had some new ideas about that.

Hoping to draw Betty from her shell, Lanza spent thousands of dollars decorating the house and grounds for Christmas. He threw open the doors for one and all—and they all came—bought gifts for everyone, strangers included, and even convinced Harry Lachmann to sell him the entire setup of cage and lovebirds that graced his entrance as a special gift for his wife. He had it delivered on Christmas day along with an expensive watch. The birds were immediately given the names Mario and Betty and, along with their dog Tenor, became a part of the house.

The new year started with conferences to prepare for a three-month tour which was being put together by Columbia Concerts.

Terry and Mario left for Palm Springs. Terry intended there to train Mario for the tour as he would a fighter. While they were away, Betty executed one of her periodic household changeovers, hiring a butler-chauffeur named Charles, who showed up with a British accent and glowing letters of reference. She was impressed with foreign accents, especially British. The house was put on a military basis, and she issued detailed instructions for running it and caring for the children.

Household Schedule

1. Breakfast for children at 8:00 A.M.; vary menu to include fresh fruit, orange juice, stewed prunes. Put honey on cooked cereals instead of sugar.

2. House to be thoroughly and generally cleaned twice a week—Monday and Friday. Furniture polished once a week, preferably on Friday, and all smudges removed daily as you dust.

3. Pick up, straighten, and dust daily. Please do not use feather duster. Check glasses and mirrors for streaks and spots.

4. Furniture pillows aired on patio once a week. Vacuum furniture and move when cleaning.

5. Dispose of garbage and trash before breakfast every morning. There is a fine for burning anything in incinerator after 10:00 A.M. Be sure trash does not accumulate in alley—keep it neat.

6. Be sure to have house cleaned (or picked up, depending on day) before errands or other duties are thought of.

7. Please remember to move furniture at least once a week when vacuuming so dust does not accumulate.

8. Dust off cars every morning, and call garage to have them washed once a week. Always check gas. Try not to let tanks get over half empty.

9. Polish silver once a week. Be sure all silver is in good condition before a party so valuable time is not consumed polishing it while guests are here to be attended to.

10. Water all plants in house once a week and oftener if soil seems dry during summer months.

11. Clean fireplace as needed. Be sure a fire is laid and ready to be lit at all times.

12. Check bathrooms daily. Be sure they are cleaned thoroughly twice a week and there should be clean towels put up each day.

13. Turn on all lights at sundown and draw curtains. Turn all lights out first thing in the morning upon arising.

14. Roll car windows up all but a crack at night so cats can't sleep in cars. Be sure bolts are on garage doors unless someone is going out.

15. All windows and doors should be locked and bolted before you retire.

16. Take ice water in chrome pitcher and 2 crystal glasses upstairs when bed is turned down.

17. Please cook Mr. and Mrs. Lanza's vegetables just before their dinner.

18. Pick up papers on front lawn by 5:30 or 6:00 each evening. There should be 4 in all.

19. Check and replace all burned-out light bulbs as you turn on lights.

20. Change linen at least twice a week—oftener if necessary.

21. Take out dirty towels daily, and replace 4 bath, 4 hand, 4 small, and 4 washcloths.

22. Be sure to put things down on a list before we run out of them so Mrs. Lanza can order. Mrs. Lanza will do all the shopping unless otherwise stated by her.

23. Clean Lovebirds' cage every other day. Replace with clean paper when you clean.

24. Take Tenor for his morning and evening walk.

25. Keep all shelves and drawers neat and clean, and replace paper as needed. Be sure all articles of the same type are together instead of spread out all over the kitchen and butler's pantry.

26. Be sure to keep all Mr. Lanza's foods in the house in quantity, such as Lynden's sliced chicken, ricotta cheese, porterhouse steaks, etc.

27. Keep accurate account of all money spent and received in the ledger book.

28. See that ash trays are emptied and things are straightened up as you pass through a room so things don't pile up.

29. See that patio is swept off and neat appearing each day.

30. Keep service porch free of empty bottles and unnecessary items.

31. Put all food away or under cover each night.

32. Put all groceries away in their proper place as they arrive.

33. Air all rooms in house as often and as long each day as you can.

34. Go about your morning routines as quietly as possible. Be especially careful of heavy footsteps and banging doors.

35. Please pick up trays as soon as you judge we are finished with them during the day or at meals.

36. Put tables away, straighten pillows, empty ash trays when necessary. Pick up as you go along when things are out of order.

37. All mail, papers, etc., lying around can be put in on Mr. Lanza's desk when cleaning up during the day.

38. When guests arrive, please greet them, take their wraps, then come right in to see if they would like any refreshments. After guests have taken a drink, remember to return and ask if they would care for a refill. Please do not leave liquor under bar on shelves except during parties.Remove and put in locked liquor cabinet because of children.

39. House lights inside on at 7:39; outside at 8:00 P.M. Remember garage, upstairs flood light, back of bar, 2 in den, and service porch.

40. Remember to pick up 4 trade papers for Mr. Lanza after you drive Colleen to nursery school.

41. Try to arrange your schedule so you can take a short nap in the afternoon.

42. Clean refrigerator well twice a week, and defrost. Throw out all old food as you go along.

43. Cook fresh vegetables for children each day. Do not reheat any of their food.

44. Children can have no sweets unless given by Mr. and Mrs. Lanza as a special treat.

45. Do not give ice cream to children more than twice a week as a dessert. Give more jello and casserole dishes.

46. Move furniture in Mrs. Lanza's bedroom each day as you clean.

47. Please do all of Mrs. Lanza's personal laundry yourself.

48. Be sure bath towels and kitchen towels are washed and put away before laundress comes.

49. Try to get upstairs to clean as soon as Mr. and Mrs. Lanza come downstairs.

Nurses for Children

1. Please ring bell for breakfast around 8:00 A.M. Keep close watch on children's food to be sure everything is not overcooked and they are getting a well-balanced diet. No sweets except as special treat given by Mr. or Mrs. Lanza.

2. Have Colleen dressed in overalls and blouse (or as weather permits, shorts or dresses) and ready for nursery school at 9:00 A.M.

3. Put Ellisa to bed with top closed and a few safe toys to play with while you eat your breakfast.

4. Dress Ellisa for morning walk after your breakfast. Be sure she has sunbonnet on if sun is hot.

5. If Ellisa becomes bored or tired on walk, bring her home to play in yard.

6. Lunch at 12:00 o'clock in nursery. Let her feed herself as much as possible, but help her along when she tires.

7. After lunch, clean Baby-tenda and floor; give baby bath, allow her time to play in tub.

8. Clean pajamas or nightie, and put down for 2 hour nap. Be sure snaps on blankets are secure and there is nothing in her crib she can choke or otherwise hurt herself on. Straighten nursery.

9. Turn on speaker before carrying lunch tray down.

10. Eat your lunch.

11. Baby gets up from nap about 3:00 P.M. Give her whole dropper of Oleum Percomorphum, a small glass of apple juice with the chill taken off, and a couple of crackers or some pretzels. No sugar cookies or other sweets.

12. Go for a short walk before Colleen gets home about 4:00 P.M.

13. Play in yard with both children until 5:30 P.M., weather permitting.

14. Dinner for both children in nursery at 5:30 P.M.

15. Put Ellisa to bed after dinner and bring Colleen downstairs for television with mother and daddy.

16. Eat your supper as close to 6:30 P.M. as you can.

17. Colleen goes to bed at 7:30 every night except when Mrs. Lanza or Mr. Lanza requests her company later.
18. If Mr. Lanza is home, he will take children up and sing to them.
19. Colleen goes potty, brushes teeth, brushes hair, reads a story of her choosing, and goes to bed. Put on little record player with Mr. Lanza's record on. Go through routine calmly but firmly.
20. Be sure speaker is on both upstairs and down when you are not with children.
21. Pick up rooms and lay clothes out the night before for in the morning.
22. Oversee diet; be sure they get a variety of well-balanced foods. Not too much ice cream and no sweets for dessert.
23. Keep nursery and Colleen's room picked up and neat as you go along so things don't pile up.
24. Air both rooms every day for as long as possible.
25. Change sheets and towels twice a week and oftener if necessary.
26. Wash baby's rubber pants and all plastic bibs every other day.
27. Polish shoes and wash shoelaces every night. Use old piece of washcloth or other rough material to make shoes shine.
28. Be sure laundress has laundry downstairs early on Tuesday and Friday mornings. Carry laundered clothes from laundry room to upstairs and put away.
29. Diaper man comes for diapers on Tuesday at 9:10 A.M. Bring dirty diaper bag downstairs and take clean ones upstairs to fold and put away.
30. Run carpet sweeper in nursery closet over rugs in between general cleanings.
31. Be sure both children get vitamins every day, and lots of liquids to drink.
32. Give Ellisa a head wash every Friday and Colleen every Saturday. There is a hair dryer in Mrs. Lanza's room and a hand dryer in your bathroom closet.
33. Be sure all toys are picked up outside and put away every night because of mildew.
34. Please do not go off the block when both children are with you. Never tell anyone who stops you on the street

69

who the children are—even if they seem to know.

35. Be sure all gates and doors are closed and/or locked in whatever room you are in with children.

36. We don't need a baby-sitter, we need a nurse. Please see that children are kept amused and entertained. They have all manner of toys, games, and books to help you.

37. Don't let children alone for one minute under any circumstances.

38. Put soiled clothing in dirty clothes hamper and fold and put away all sweaters at night.

Betty had these orders posted in the kitchen and several other places in the house. When Mario looked them over, he shook his head in disbelief: "When we were kids, life was different. We didn't have so much. With all the people we have in this big house I guess Betty needs a system or we'll have problems every day. The help should know exactly what she wants."

Mario returned to Beverly Hills to start the tour. Sam Weiler, Costa, the Lanzas, and Terry boarded the train at Pasadena with dozens of suitcases and thousands of souvenir programs. Boy Scouts were hired along the way and were paid a nickel for every program they sold at each concert. After his performance Lanza, like a little boy, would wait for Terry to arrive at the hotel and empty bags of money from the program sales on the bed.

The tour had begun with a near disaster. While packing to leave, Mario said to Terry, "You take care of the music. Keep your eyes on it."

Betty said, "Hold on a minute. I'm capable of doing something. I'll take care of it." Terry turned the task over to her. Once they were in their private railroad car and headed out of Los Angeles, Mario asked Terry to bring him the music suitcase. He wanted to study some of the songs.

Terry went to Betty to ask her where the music was. She said, "What are you talking about? I don't know anything about his music. Do I look like his secretary?"

It was obvious she had been drinking, and it finally dawned on Terry that she had left the music behind. He quickly wired Mary to look for it, and the music case arrived barely in time for the first concert.

Betty wanted so much to be a part of everything Mario did that she made commitments she either couldn't—or forgot to—keep. She insisted on taking over the duty of answering fan mail. "I want to keep in touch with Mario's public." Instead the household staff found sacks of unopened mail stuffed into closets and hidden away in cabinets. Lanza finally hired two girls to handle the task.

So much money flowed in from ticket sales (not to mention the income from programs) that the tour was dubbed by Mario's close associates as "The Lanza Bonanza." *Variety* chronicled, "Lanza proves hottest draw with $177,720 gross in 22 concerts." In the early Fifties it was an unheard-of figure.

The tour began officially from their headquarters at the St. Moritz Hotel in New York. One night, shortly after their arrival, Mario and Terry were alone in Lanza's suite overlooking Central Park. As the two men stood looking out at the street below, Terry mentioned that as a kid he and his friends had been chased away by the doorman of the hotel because they weren't dressed "classy enough" to hang around in front of the St. Moritz.

Indignantly, Lanza said, "Oh yeah? Well, watch what I think of their class." He unzipped his trousers and urinated out the window. Terry joined him in the act and both roared with delight at their unorthodox method of "getting even."

The thing Lanza disliked most about touring was the incredible disrespect for his person and privacy. His clothes were torn, his hair pulled out. Kids climbed the fire escapes and tried to enter his bedroom. The realization that the surging crowds could lead to injury, either to himself or someone else, caused him more than once to cancel autograph parties and newspaper interviews. This violent adulation didn't happen just in a big city like New York but in every place he appeared.

Lanza felt trapped. Everybody else in his party could relax, go to a movie, shop, take a leisurely walk—but not him. He couldn't even go down to the hotel lobby for a newspaper.

Occasionally he and Terry would don their disguises, wait until midnight, and then slip out through the basement to get some fresh air. They would reenter the hotel by the same route.

One time Mario broke his own rule about going out in the daytime. It was in St. Petersburg, Florida, on a Sunday when no concert was scheduled. The Giants and Red Sox were having an exhibition game at Al Lang Field and Lanza wanted to go out to the ball park. "No one knows me here, I'm sure," he said.

Terry agreed reluctantly. "This is a place where old people come to retire. They might not recognize you."

In the cab on the way to the ball game Mario took a deep breath and said "Fresh air—I'm free again—and in the daylight." Nevertheless he had taken the precaution of wearing dark glasses and a floppy hat.

Terry purchased the tickets and followed a group of elderly patrons in. So far, so good. Even the people-wise cabbie hadn't recognized him.

Everything went well until the second inning, when a middle-aged matron sitting behind them leaned over and tapped him on the shoulder. "Pardon me," she asked, "but aren't you that singer—Mario Lanza?"

Without thinking Lanza said, "Yes. But I'd really like to watch the ball game." Terry wished he had denied it but it was too late. By the fifth inning Mario had signed numerous autographs, been photographed and was sweating profusely. His fingers were ink-stained and cramped from writing his name and personal messages. Finally he had had enough and he and Terry escaped.

In the cab on the way back Lanza shook his head and scowled at Terry. "You lucky son-of-a-bitch! You could sit there and see the game, enjoy the sun, and nobody bothered you. I'd trade places with you in a minute."

His complaints notwithstanding, he never forgot to ask how much money Terry took in from the program sales, and at intermission he would always say, "Go back out there and you'll sell twice as many after the show." He made sure of this by giving a little speech at the end of each show, plugging his new movie, winding up with an encore of "Be My Love," and urging people to buy the program. He was in a trap of his own devising. He reveled in public acceptance too much to seriously consider renouncing it.

It pleased him immensely that he inspired an adulation which had previously been given only to popular crooners such as Frank Sinatra. "Be My Love" incited sighs and screams reminiscent of the bobby-soxers who daily invaded New York's Paramount Theatre during the early Forties.

He could be very charming with his fans, too, in spite of the invasions on his privacy. Once in Pittsburgh a teenage girl managed to sneak into his suite. He was so patient and kind to her that she later moved to California and became vice-president of the Mario Lanza fan club.

Outrageous clowning remained Lanza's primary way of blowing off steam on the tour. At one stop Manny Sachs of RCA was coming to dinner. Lanza had Terry and his friend George Eiferman (Mr. America) strip and put bath towels around their waists and heads to look like slaves.

When Sachs arrived, the muscular Eiferman opened the door. "I beg your pardon," Sachs said, "I must have the wrong room."

In a bass voice Eiferman said, "Follow me. The master waits."

Sachs followed him into the room where Mario and Betty jumped from behind a chair, yelling "Surprise!" Even the highest paid executive at RCA Victor did not escape the Lanza humor.

In Philadelphia Mario was handed a piece of paper by a

total stranger as he waited for the elevator to take him to his floor. Upstairs he asked Sam Weiler, "What's this?"

Sam read it and said, "You're being sued. A voice teacher by the name of Mrs. Arthur E. I. Jackson says she gave you singing lessons at the rate of $5.00 per week when you were an unknown and you have breached your contract with her."

"She's crazy," Mario replied.

Not so crazy, as it turned out. Mrs. Jackson was Irene Williams, his old voice coach. The agreement had been signed in 1942 just before Lanza left for Tanglewood. Mario, according to the paper, had agreed to pay her five percent of his earnings in excess of $5,000 a year and ten percent of earnings in excess of $7,500.

In his excitement about going to study with Koussevitzky, Lanza had signed the agreement without reading it. It was typical of him not to want to be bothered reading contracts; that was why he had given Weiler power of attorney to sign his name. In this particular case he was lucky to get off with a $10,000 settlement. The legal summons was doubly annoying, having been served in his home town. It was an especially important stop on the tour.

On the day of his performance no visitors were allowed to see him. Naturally his friends and family were upset; Terry and Sam bore the brunt of their criticism.

That night Lanza was nervous, pacing back and forth in his hotel suite before it was time to leave for the concert. He was doing only one show, although the promoters had tried to get him to do more. Arriving at the Academy of Music, he and his entourage were ushered backstage, where 400 additional seats had been set up.

The entire Lanza clan had front orchestra seats, except for Grandma Lanza, who was home ill. "Terry," he said, "I've been told that many of my friends may have no tickets. Try to sneak them in backstage." Terry was able to sneak in a few before the police refused to allow any more, because of fire hazard.

Lanza sang without a microphone. During the first half of

74

the program he faced out front. After the intermission he came on stage. "Ladies and gentlemen, all evening the people behind me have been looking at my back. Do you mind if I turn around and sing to them?" He then sang to the people who had been crowded in behind him. Marion Kelley of the *Philadelphia Inquirer* summed it up the following day: "Mario Lanza came home last night . . . and the old Academy of Music has not seen or heard such applause for a singer in many a day."

The success of the tour was marred by rumors of an impending separation between Mario and Betty. Their fights, fueled by alcohol (and in Betty's case, drugs) were becoming more violent. Lamps, vases, and other articles of furniture were frequently broken. In the heat of battle Betty would accuse Mario of being a mama's boy. "Everybody knows you love *her* more than you do me!" she said once. "I'll bet a psychiatrist would have a ball with that one!"

Dorothy Kilgallen wrote: "It won't be long before the Mario Lanzas are forced to yodel denials of a rift." Betty blamed the help for leaking information to the press and fired them wholesale. But the gossip persisted, and for good reason.

Meanwhile the tour was doing great business. In Miami one night the air-conditioning failed. With his usual way with an audience, Lanza put everyone at ease.

"Isn't this a beautiful auditorium? I took my basic training here in Miami. I'm sorry the air-conditioning isn't working and you're all uncomfortable. Tell you what, ladies, take your shoes off. Men, unbutton your ties. I'll loosen mine and we'll relax and I'll sing for you."

In Fresno, California, the last stop on the tour, Lanza, in a mellow mood, said to Terry: "You know, I never really see my audience up close. Let's get a cab and drive by the hall and look at the people going in."

The cab was parked across the street. Lanza, sitting in the back seat, noticed people on crutches and in wheelchairs. "Go tell the manager to put those people in the front of the line."

He watched with delight as his request was fulfilled. He was completely awed by his fame, but there was also an undeniable sense of insecurity, as if he couldn't quite believe it.

While the tour was in progress "Be My Love" went over the million mark, the first time a singer on Red Seal Victor Label had accomplished this feat, and Lanza's recording of "The Loveliest Night of the Year" became a top-selling single.

Betty, living increasingly in the shadow of her husband and liking it less, detested the luncheons and "ladies' affairs" she had to attend. "I'm just your flunky," she protested. "You get all the credit and I'm the one who has to listen to a bunch of old hens cackle and fawn about my husband. I have feelings, too!"

Back in Los Angeles Lanza frolicked with his children and ignored his wife's withdrawal to the bedroom again. He had resigned himself to Betty's problems. "She is the mother of my children," he told Terry shortly after their return. "If she wants to spend the rest of her life in bed, that's her business. I have to think about the children and what is best for them. *They* are my future, not my wife."

IO

Like many entertainers, Lanza had ambivalent feelings about the press. He resented the exaggerated and often untrue items that were printed about him. At the same time he wooed the press—publicity, after all, was the name of the game. Naturally the members of the press came in for some of his practical jokes.

One evening, shortly after his return to California, he invited a group of newsmen over for a drink. Mary happened to be there, in the bedroom with the children. "Have Mom fix her hair and tell her she's a famous movie actress from Italy," Lanza suggested to Terry. "We'll have some fun with these guys."

Mary was told she should speak Italian and a little broken English—Mario would handle the rest. During the interview, he said, "Boys, I have a real exclusive for you. I brought a famous Italian movie star to America who will be appearing with me in my next film. She's staying with Betty and me and I'd like you to meet her."

When Mary entered everybody rose and Lanza introduced her. Betty said, "Maria speaks mostly Italian, but Mario will help translate for you."

One of the reporters asked, "How will you handle her lack of English in a film?"

Mario thought quickly. "She's playing an Italian girl who falls in love with me. I teach her English in the picture. It's a comedy."

Mary sat posing for pictures and enjoying every minute of the interview until a reporter who had made a few too many trips to the bar began to close in on her. As he was about to place a hand on her knee, Lanza jumped up! "Hey, get your hands off my mother! That's my Mom!" It was hard for them to believe; since Mary looked so young, people often mistook her and Mario for brother and sister.

Lanza was mischievous and full of fun, and people liked to be around him. Nobody could light up a room as he did. But sometimes he didn't know when to stop. He couldn't find a comfortable middle ground between the devoted family man that he was much of the time and the wild man who would stop at no outrageous behavior.

During the period following the three-month tour he had a brief affair with an actress who was twenty years older than he was. He soon tired of her and decided to end it.

The two of them were pretty well loaded one night and Terry was driving them around Hollywood. Lanza began to tell the actress about a game he played as a boy in South Philadelphia. "Did you ever play 'Fire in the church'?" he asked.

"No, Mario. How does it go?"

"Let's say you're the church and you're on fire." He promptly unzipped his fly, let fly a stream of urine, and said, "That ought to put out *your* fire. Terry, take me home."

The Great Caruso premiered on the night of May 29, 1951. A studio limousine picked up Lanza and his family. Film maker Jesse Lasky also rode with them at Mario's request. It had been Lasky's idea for him to play Caruso.

The forecourt of the Hollywood Egyptian Theatre had been redecorated to represent the 1905 of Caruso's first visit to America. It was like a red plush opera house illuminated by gas lights. Even the one-sheet billboards were reminiscent of those days.

The reviews were terrific, from the *Mirror News*'s "Caruso renders unto Lanza his own voice," to Louella Parsons' "Mario

Lanza's voice so beautiful, so great is worthy of Caruso . . . be proud that motion pictures have made this possible with as great an artist as Mario Lanza."

Mario's old friend and mentor, Dr. Peter Herman Adler, now NBC's opera chief, was not so quick to compare Lanza with Caruso. "Ask me again in ten years. It took Caruso that long to become a successful singer. Today, we don't know where Lanza will land."

A major ladies magazine sent a writer out from New York to interview Mario. A very chic, demure, Bryn Mawr type, she was no match for Mario's chicanery. After two days of probing questions and having her photographer snap Mario in the most candid situations, he insisted on treating her to lunch prior to her return to New York.

Over dessert he smiled warmly. "Now dear," he asked pleasantly, "you've asked me questions for two days; may I please ask one of you?" His boyish manner was disarming.

"Of course," she said. "Anything you wish."

Staring deeply into her eyes and in a very warm, clear voice, he asked, "Do you give good head?"

Feigning a smile she nervously replied, "If we don't hurry I'll miss my plane."

In the car as Terry drove him home he said, "She'll never forget me and I'll get a great story." He was right—it was a great story.

Lanza was soaring. Coca-Cola sought him to replace Edgar Bergen for a summer radio show. *Variety* announced that many classical singers were responding to the sales of "Be My Love" by rushing to their recording studios to wax popular tunes. With Broadway shows doing so-so business, *Variety* gave Lanza another push with this banner headline: BROADWAY ON SKIDS, BUT CARUSO SMASH. *The Great Caruso*, at the end of the first nine weeks, had played to 1,245,000 people, breaking the current record for Radio City Music Hall in New York. No other film, regardless of how long it ran, had grossed higher.

The Coca-Cola show became a reality. Terry drove Lanza to the CBS studios in Hollywood for the first Sunday Night Show. The crowds were so large they had difficulty getting to the entrance. Lanza ordered, "No more audiences. We'll tape the show in another studio in the future."

In his review of the show Jack Mabley of the Chicago *Daily News* wrote: "Even if you get tired of Lanza's record, "Be My Love," or even if you lean toward the Crosby kind of hooting, you should try Mr. Lanza's singing for half an hour. It's quite a thrill. How any human can sing so loud and clear without blowing a tonsil is a secret only Lanza can tell....Gisele MacKenzie was a guest on the show and it's brutal to any singer to put him or her on the same half-hour with Mario Lanza."

On June 27, 1951, RCA Victor presented a gold record to Lanza for "Be My Love," the biggest selling single classical record by a vocalist in the company's history. Among those at the presentation in Hollywood were Mario's parents and family, and Ray Sinatra (Frank's cousin) who did the arrangement for the recording. An inanimate but audible witness was Tony Cocozza's ancient Victrola on which Mario had listened to Caruso records as a boy.

Against the better judgment of his advisors, he posed with Hedda Hopper when he received the gold record. The studio publicity people, anxious to give even treatment to Hopper and Louella Parsons, Hollywood's unofficial czars of publicity, objected.

"The hell with them," Lanza said. "I promised Hedda the day I broke her mirror." The story, undoubtedly apocryphal, was that he had once told Hopper he could rock a cup and saucer and shatter a mirror with one of his high notes.

Dubious, Hopper said, "Try it."

Taking the stance of a fighter, he opened his mouth and let fly a high note like a cannonball. As he had promised (so the story went), the corner of the framed mirror in the room cracked.

It was the end of his love affair with Louella Parsons. She

began to find fault with Lanza and every time the opportunity came, she did a hatchet job on him. To pose with Hedda and omit her was blasphemy.

Mario lost his most valuable friend when Louis B. Mayer decided to step down as head of MGM and was replaced by Dore Schary. Mario was not one of Mr. Schary's favorites as he rather plainly states in his recent autobiography, and Mario soon found out that Schary would never become the father image to him that Mr. Mayer had been.

Lanza had become too successful to listen to advice. It wasn't necessarily a matter of acquiring a big head. Lanza, like many successful artists, had a sure sense of what was right for him. But the bouts of temperament were trying to everyone around him.

Terry watched closely when he sang, looking for signs of strain or illness. He always had hot tea with honey in a thermos ready for the end of the song. Lanza insisted that a jigger of scotch be added to the tea. If it wasn't, he would pout like a baby and hold up the recording session, wasting musicians' and technicians' time and giving executives ulcers. Then without warning he would jauntily shout, "Okay, boys, let's cut a record!"

After a recording session he would take Terry aside and ask, "How was it?" They would go to the control room and listen to the playback. Lanza relived every line as he listened, and seldom was he overjoyed with the results. As others swooned and applauded, he would shake his head and say, "I should have done better."

Lanza continued to give parties which often found him singing into the predawn hours without letup. At the same time his refusal to warble a note at the parties of Hollywood's top executives was cited as another example of his being temperamental.

Hedda Hopper, getting wind of the anti-Lanza gossip, threw down the gauntlet to MGM. "These cracks against Mario Lanza are being handed out by higher-ups at his own studio. You know why? He won't sing for free at their parties. Looks as if Mario, whose *Caruso* is one of the biggest grosses Metro ever had, is being punished for bringing home the bacon."

The so-called "little people" at the studio—carpenters, electricians, extras—lined up behind Lanza in the developing feud. He was regarded as one of them, and whenever he came on the lot he was surrounded by the workers who understood the wrath that could come down from "upstairs."

Betty had no "little people" to comfort her. She was never really well after Ellisa's birth and the strain of the last tour. She found a masseuse who came to the house twice a week and who was a self-proclaimed authority on every subject from medicine to politics. Betty fell under her spell because the lady gave her the pills she asked for to "relax." When her doctor found out about it he got rid of the medication *and* the masseuse.

Lanza was drinking more than ever and he no longer tried to keep his woman-chasing a secret. That task fell to Terry, who had his hands full protecting him from blackmail or extortion, as well as from Betty's wrath and possible divorce. Lanza kept him up practically every night, drinking and partying with women. He promised them all parts in his movies and Terry ran around with a pencil and pad taking down names and addresses. He didn't keep his promises, and the women who made a fuss were paid off in cash, often as much as a thousand dollars.

Old friends and associates such as Sam Weiler began to stay away and a new breed appeared on the scene, notably friends of Nick Brodszky whom Lanza referred to as "The Gypsies," because they were Hungarian. There was constant backbiting among the group. They all knew Joe Pasternak, also Hungarian, and were jealous of his relationship with Lanza. They talked to Mario about Pasternak, to Pasternak about Brodszky, and—Lanza assumed—to both men about him. Petty gossip had never been a part of his life but now he got enjoyment from it, and he was also quick to argue with anybody for little or no reason.

Lanza went after MGM demanding more dramatic roles and threatening to quit acting if he didn't get them. "I can sing on any concert stage in the world," he said. "I don't need motion pictures."

He was overruled and told to abide by his contract. That meant he had to obey the Metro lion just as every other contract star was compelled to do. *Because You're Mine* would be his next assignment. He would do it and like it.

Lanza made up his mind from the beginning not to be cooperative on the film. "I'll let them see what it means to deal with a difficult star. Gable is a lamb. I'm the *real* lion." Terry shuddered at the implications.

Someone at MGM leaked word to Ed Sullivan, who, in addition to hosting a weekly television show, wrote a daily column in the New York *Daily News*. The following item appeared: "Temperamental antics of Mario Lanza driving MGM daffy. The studio never having met a performer so incapable of handling success."

Lanza commented, "Now that's the first time Ed Sullivan ever picked on me. I wonder how he would feel if he were asked to do his column everywhere he went, as I am asked to sing." It went right past Mario that Sullivan's item related to his conduct at the studio and not his refusal to sing at some producer's bash.

Dorothy Manners, the syndicated Hollywood columnist, picked up where Sullivan left off. MGM was preparing the world for a break between the studio and Lanza. Everything was aimed at making the rift appear to be totally his fault, not the studio's. That wasn't entirely true. Lanza wanted and deserved better parts. He knew how wasted Lauritz Melchior's talents had been at the same studio in silly pictures that had no real value. The great Metropolitan Opera star was made to look like a buffoon in Esther Williams swimoramas. Lanza desperately wanted to avoid that.

Manners, who was associated with Louella Parsons, sided with the studio. "What's with Mario Lanza? Latest is that he wants out of his MGM contract instead of just handing them a few headaches from his recently developed temperament. They're really spending money on his pictures even in these times of retrenchment . . . the studio that started him and put him over is entitled to cash in, too."

Manners' information came from Joe Pasternak and was based on his conversation with Lanza about the *Because You're Mine* assignment. Pasternak said, "Mario, I plan to present you in a light musical comedy about an opera singer who is drafted into the Army, becomes involved in funny situations and problems, falls in love, then becomes adjusted and the picture has a happy ending."

Lanza had rebelled. "I don't like your idea, Joe. I want a big lavish musical, a costume type film with a lot of great music—like bringing grand opera to the screen." He argued that teenagers loved his concerts and "they now love opera."

Betty, happy to be involved in one of her husband's decisions, agreed with him. Mario complained to Sam, who said he would discuss it with Pasternak. Adding fuel to the fire, Nick Brodszky and two of his pals came over to Lanza's that evening to console him. They denounced Pasternak and one of them, a man we'll call Harry, went so far as to tell Lanza that he was "bigger than the studio." "They should," he said, "rename the place Metro-Goldwyn-Mario." Lanza poured him another glass of champagne and listened as Harry explained a plan to defeat the studio.

Terry, sensing that Lanza might be taking the guy too seriously, told him to shut up. Harry complained to Lanza, "The gangster is threatening me." (That group all called Terry "Mario's gangster.")

Lanza laughed. "Look out for Terry. He carries a good left hook."

Betty yelled from upstairs as the boys became more boisterous. "Shut up down there! I'm trying to sleep."

Lanza, not wanting a fight, said, "Harry, get out. Betty doesn't like you. She doesn't want you around."

The man laughed weakly and tried to joke. "If your wife chases me out, I'll pitch a tent and sleep on your lawn."

Nick got his boys together and they left. Afterward Terry asked Lanza why he allowed Nick to bring those guys around.

Harry was a photographer and once almost gave Lanza more than a few laughs. At his apartment one night he produced a stunning model for Mario's pleasure. While Lanza and the model were in the bedroom, he and Terry nursed drinks in the living room. Harry excused himself to go to the bathroom. Terry, wondering why he was gone so long, went to look and found him at the keyhole trying to get some shots with his camera. Terry was so angry he broke the camera and hustled Mario out of the place.

Joe Pasternak had no idea what was going on between his fellow-countrymen and Lanza. If he had, he would not have blamed Mario for some of their personal differences during the filming of *Because You're Mine*. There were signs, too, that Lanza himself was troubled by his behavior.

He confided to Terry, "For the first time in my life, I find myself walking alone for hours I can't stand to have anybody near me. I have to be by myself. I'm nervous and jittery. Betty's the most wonderful girl in the world and she understands me. It's not fair to her. The people who work for me have it rough sometimes, too. I take my worries out on them."

Certainly Lanza's behavior in both his personal and professional life was often lamentable. His success had been too big and had come too quickly for him to handle, and he and his wife were paying the price. The tragedy was that Lanza's gift was unique, a beautiful voice combined with a larger than life personality. He had worked hard and sincerely to make the most of this gift, but his faults unfortunately were as large as his virtues. He had started out, as one observer put it, as "an eager ingenuous boy bubbling over with native warmth."

Somewhere along the way the eager ingenuous boy had become lost.

II

The eyes of the world were focused on the Korean War during the summer of 1951, when *Time* magazine ran a cover story on Lanza entitled "Million Dollar Voice" in its August 6 issue. Notwithstanding the prestige of appearing on *Time*'s cover, the story was far from flattering. Beneath a comical caricature of Lanza with a diminutive Enrico Caruso in the background, painted by Boris Chaliapin, son of the great Russian bass singer, Feodor Chaliapin, the cover featured a pointed blurb: "Would Caruso fracture 'em in Scranton?"

The first paragraph manufactured a vanity far beyond any Lanza had ever displayed. "Oh Mario," it had him exclaiming in self-admiration, "you can sing like a son-of-a-bitch!" The story went on to exaggerate every vice and indiscretion he had ever been accused of.

"He once ran out of his studio dressing room clad only in an athletic supporter and raced hilariously around the set, while girls fled in all directions." His "literary tastes" were said to run to body-building and fan magazines.

What hurt even more was that an old friend, Johnny Silver, was quoted at length about his relationship with Lanza in the early days. "His shirt was open, he didn't have a hat, no laces in his shoes, he hadn't taken a bath in six months," so said Silver. "He hadn't taken his socks off in six months and the guy weighed 287 pounds."

Dropping the magazine, Mario looked at Betty and asked, "What did he do that to me for?"

During all the years that Terry knew him, Lanza had a fetish about cleanliness, often showering several times a day. He never weighed more than 240 pounds, at which point he simply *looked* monstrous due to his massive chest. He had been made to look like a yodeling hillbilly.

Some columnists were as distressed as he was. Mike Connolly in the *Hollywood Reporter* said *Time* had missed the real story. "For instance, the wonderful new world Lanza has opened to millions who had never heard of *Pagliacci*. . . ." Jack Lait in the New York *Mirror* called the article one of *Time's* "roughest."

Perhaps it was the *Time* cover story. Whatever the reason, Lanza seemed to take stock of his life and see where it was leading. He and Betty went on a long vacation to Oregon and for a while their marriage was happy and serene. But it didn't last. The pressures and temptations of being a superstar, before the term was even coined, were too great, and after his return to California, Lanza was soon back to his old ways.

He resumed his feud with MGM, going on a deliberate eating binge which caused the studio to postpone the picture and send Doretta Morrow, who was to be his leading lady (fresh from the Broadway hit *The King and I*), back to New York to await notice that the film was ready to start.

He brought his troubles with the studio home, and before long the Lanzas were battling again. "Listen to me," he shouted during one fight. "You are not the star. I am. It is my face and my voice that pays for all of this." He waved his arms dramatically. "The studio is trying to ruin me. If I am ruined we will lose everything!"

"Good!" Betty screamed. "Then maybe we can go back to living like normal people!" She jumped up and ran to her bedroom and slammed the door.

The domestic scene wasn't helped by continued sniping by the press. Lanza blamed the studio for the malicious gossip.

But Howard Strickling, MGM's publicity director, offered a thousand dollars if he could prove any of the items had come from Metro.

As an almost comical addition to the flak he was getting, a storm was brewing in Italy over MGM's advertising campaign for *The Great Caruso*. The Italian countryside was plastered with billboards and posters heralding the coming attraction. Unfortunately, the ads also plugged Technicolor, Coca-Cola (Lanza's radio sponsor), and a singing contest tie-in. The ads so angered Caruso's son and grandson that they took it to court and asked for a ban on the ads. The courts sided with the Carusos and, although it was too late to take down all the signs, alterations were immediately ordered. These, however, left something to be desired. What remained of the original poster were the words "Coca-Cola" and the body of the singer—who had been decapitated in the process.

Part of Lanza's generosity was showing off, of course. But part of it was undeniably genuine. As a big star, he was in a position to do a lot of favors and inevitably people took advantage of him. Inevitably, too, his success stirred jealousy.

One of the regulars at Lanza's house was a music conductor. After a successful career, the conductor was having difficulty finding a good job. He had asked Lanza if he could be the conductor for one of his RCA recording sessions.

One night Lanza brought up his name and said, "I think I'll use him on my next session. As a matter of fact, let's stop by his house and tell him it's set."

"How do you know RCA will go for it?" Terry asked. Mario—like a little boy with his hand behind his back who suddenly thrusts out a bouquet of flowers for mom—smiled. "I know. I cleared it with Manny Sachs today."

Terry shook his head in amusement.

"Why don't we pick up a pizza and go over to his house. We'll celebrate Italian style." When they arrived at the conductor's home in West Los Angeles the lights were out. Lanza said, "C'mon around back. Maybe they're still up."

Sure enough, a light was on in the upstairs bedroom window, which was open. Loud voices could be heard.

The wife was shouting, "Don't jump just because Mario Lanza is a big shot. You're an artist. He's only a flash. He won't last. He's trying to make everyone like him."

"Let's get out of here," Terry said.

Lanza shook his head. "No, I want to hear."

The wife went on. "That's why he feeds so many people in his home. And another thing, don't drag me over there anymore. All we do is listen to him and his records. You're talented. You don't have to get on your knees and beg him for anything. Lanza needs *you*. You don't need him. And that nagging wife of his. . . ."

Lanza stood below listening to the woman's appraisal of him and his family. Finally he threw the pizza on the lawn in disgust and said, "Let's get out of here. Now I know why he boozes so much. If I had a wife like that I'd booze, too."

The conductor never knew why Lanza didn't return any of his calls—and Mario never bothered to explain.

Not all the generous gestures went unappreciated, though. Shortly after the Lanzas' return from Oregon, Terry took a long-distance call from a hospital in New Jersey. A woman asked for Mario. Terry said, "He's out, but I'll be glad to pass along any message." The woman's daughter was ten years old and dying of leukemia. Her one wish was to meet Mario Lanza. She had written a letter and received no reply. The woman apologized for any intrusion. Terry took down the name and hospital and promised she would hear from Lanza.

Mario was afraid it was a crank call. "But what if it's true?" he said. "Think of the poor kid ten years old with cancer. I'll have to find out. I couldn't sleep if I didn't. Get her on the phone, Terry. Let's see what it's all about."

The telephone operator at the hospital couldn't believe it when the call came in. "I never thought a big movie star would care about a kid thousands of miles away," she later told reporters. Lanza talked with young Raphaela Fasano for several minutes. "I have two little girls just like you," he said.

"I know their names," she replied, "Colleen and Ellisa." Betty got on the phone and talked with Raphaela, who assured her she was feeling fine. "Right now," she said, "I'm on top of the world."

Lanza promised that he would sing "Tina Lina" from *The Toast of New Orleans* on his next radio show and that the show would be dedicated to her.

Some time before Christmas Lanza received a call from Raphaela's mother. Her daughter was near death but the doctors were allowing her to have an early Christmas party at home. The call came in as Lanza and Ray Sinatra were going over a song Sinatra had written for *Because You're Mine*, called "Lee-ah-Loo." They dropped their work and, with Sinatra accompanying him, Lanza sang "Silent Night" for Raphaela.

He arranged to have her flown to Hollywood for a visit. Lanza, Betty, Sam, Jack Keller, Lanza's parents, and Terry were at the airport to greet the little girl. Mario gave her a welcoming kiss and embraced her warmly. Raphaela was given the star treatment with a shopping tour, accompanied by Betty and Colleen, lunch at MGM studios, where stars such as Jimmy Stewart, Lana Turner, and Ricardo Montalban showed up to be photographed with her. The visit culminated with a big party in her honor.

Raphaela went home a very happy girl. She lived another eighteen months and died quietly in her sleep. She was buried with a gold cross that Mario sent her, along with his picture.

Lanza understood the influence of a star on the young far better than his critics understood him.

Lanza's summer show was so successful that Coca-Cola renewed it on a permanent basis and Gisele MacKenzie, who had been his first guest, was signed as a regular.

The prerecording sessions for *Because You're Mine* went smoothly. Nick Brodszky and Sammy Cahn wrote the title song. Irving Aaronson and Paul Francis Webster contributed "The Song Angels Sing" and Ray Sinatra, collaborating with

Johnny Leemans, provided "Lee-ah-Loo." The score also included "Addio alla Madre" from *Cavalleria rusticana*, "Mamma mia, che vo' sape?" "You Do Something to Me," "Granada," "The Lord's Prayer," and a few other short operatic numbers.

Lanza's Christmas album had sold 240,000 copies in the first week and was on its way to becoming the most successful Christmas album ever recorded.

The world was spinning around Lanza. He had no real sense of direction. Nothing seemed to be working for him except the cash register—and that worked in both directions. The money came in, the money went out. Making and spending money seemed to be the only fun he had. Betty withdrew into herself again. She had difficulty sleeping at night and couldn't stay awake in the daytime. Her doctor had refused to prescribe sleeping pills because of their adverse effect on her. Nevertheless she managed to get them.

One afternoon Lanza was having a conversation with Terry in the living room. "I'm going for a walk outside for a little air," he said.

His voice sounded strange and Terry, concerned, said, "I'll go with you."

"No, no," Lanza said. "I'll go by myself. You sit here and watch television."

When he returned after a moment his breath smelled of whiskey. Terry said nothing but later slipped outside and made a search of the grounds, turning up several bottles. It was a disturbing turn in Lanza's drinking habits.

Around this time Terry was called into the MGM executive offices and given a talking to. Get Lanza off the food and booze. It was an order although MGM was no longer paying Terry's salary. But he shared the studio's concern and told the front office he would try.

His attempts went unrewarded. Mario would tell him, "Get the hell out of here. Go to the movies. Go home. I'll take care of myself." Whenever Terry left him, though, Lanza invariably got into trouble. He was, as Louis B. Mayer had often said, a little boy who shouldn't be left alone for more than a few minutes. Like a spoiled child, he did all the attention-getting things that spoiled children do: he overate, overdrank, would give some strange girl all of his money or promise her a part in his next movie. He could also be mean when he drank. He never intended to do bad things, he would always explain to Terry after some escapade, he simply couldn't control himself.

Although Betty grew jealous of Terry because he spent so much time with her husband, she wanted him to be there; he was a necessary evil. Tony and Mary, on the other hand, begged Terry to stay close to their son, a son they were understanding less and less as his success increased.

Whatever Lanza did after dark, he was on the *Because You're Mine* set in the morning. In the picture he played a Metropolitan Opera star who is drafted into the Army. Doretta Morrow had returned from New York and a young comic, Bobby Van, was making his screen debut. Van cracked jokes on the set and could break Lanza up. He became a stabilizing factor in an uneasy situation.

As he had in the past, Lanza insisted that Mary and Tony appear in a scene. "Someday my mother and father will be gone. It'll be good for their grandchildren to see what they were really like."

Terry had a part in the picture, too, as one of Lanza's Army buddies, and he staged a fight scene between Mario and actor James Whitmore. An ex-boxer from Brooklyn named Mickey Golden was Lanza's stand-in. Golden had been around pictures for 28 years as a bit player. When the movie was finished, Mario put him on salary and he became a part of what some people were calling "Lanza's Repertoire Company." Mario hired anybody he took a liking to. The bookkeepers in his manager's office were driven crazy by the constant additions and changes to the weekly payroll.

His generosity on at least one occasion got him in trouble with the studio. An ex-boxer, Abie Bain, got into a hassle on the set and was removed from the picture. When Lanza heard about it he called in the assistant director and said, "I heard about Abie Bain being let go. I want him back on the picture. I'll be responsible for him. Just put him back on salary." The executives in the front office grumbled and it was shortly leaked to the press that Lanza was trying to run the studio.

The *Because You're Mine* set was like a mine field where an explosion could happen any minute. Lanza had always had sensitive ears. Loud noises gave him a headache. Everybody at the studio knew it, but somebody obviously forgot. One afternoon on the large indoor sound stage they were shooting. a scene that involved military maneuvers. A small group of actors, including Lanza, were down on all fours creeping up a hill. Suddenly they received a signal from the director, Al Hall, to stand up and fire their rifles. Nobody told them they were too close to Lanza. The gunfire caused him to scream out and grab his ears as he rolled on the ground in pain. The doctor ordered him home to bed for two days.

The daily press cited the incident as another of the "problems" that plagued the picture.

Modern Screen notified Lanza that in a worldwide poll he was voted most popular male singer. The magazine threw a big party at Ciro's to present the award. The press turned out. Metro-Goldwyn-Mayer top executives were noticeably absent. So was Lanza. The press was critical of him. None of the critics bothered to call Lanza's home to ask why he didn't show.

He had had the day off from the studio. He, Betty, and Terry were lounging in the den reading the morning papers when Marion Rigsbee, the maid, came in puffing with excitement. "Something is wrong with Tenor. You better hurry."

They found the family dog frothing at the mouth, a very sick animal. Mario and Terry managed to wrap it in a terry cloth bath towel and they all ran to the garage. Terry jumped into the driver's seat and backed the car out. On the way to the veterinarian he ignored all traffic signals and that soon brought a motorcycle officer alongside. Terry frantically motioned to the back seat. Betty was yelling, "My baby! My baby!" The

93

policeman, mistaking Tenor for an infant, escorted the car and didn't realize his error until they arrived at the animal hospital.

Tenor died within an hour. Betty promptly fainted. The confused policeman offered sympathy and helped Lanza and Terry get her back into the car. If the incident hadn't been so upsetting, it would have made a good Marx Brothers picture.

Terry suggested that Jack Keller issue a statement explaining why Mario hadn't attended the *Modern Screen* cocktail party. "Are you kidding?" Lanza said. "They'd never believe it."

By the end of the year, however shaky Lanza's personal life might be, his professional life couldn't have been better.

The *Atlanta Journal and Constitution* thanked Judge Medina and the Supreme Court "for crushing America's Commie leaders," Bobby Thomson for "giving us the biggest home run thrill in years," and Mario Lanza's voice "for the top movie moment of the year in *The Great Caruso*."

The *Independent Film Journal* presented him with his second annual award in a row as the year's top money-making actor. "This was my year," he boasted, "and I'd like to end it with a bang." He had something special in mind. On his year-end radio show he decided to sing the English lyrics to "La donna è mobile." Opera purists were disdainful but Lanza said, "I only wish there were suitable English lyrics to more of the world's great operas. I believe the American people have a deep and intuitive appreciation for great music and respond enthusiastically whenever it is presented straightforwardly without any arty pretentiousness and in intelligible form.

"I'd like to see opera become as popular in this country as jazz, and I like good jazz, too. People are finding out that opera can be fun." He received compliments for his performance from hundreds of fans.

The Great Caruso was the top film of the year. The London *Daily Mirror* commented on Lanza's sex appeal: "100 million women thrilled by one man's voice!" RCA announced that

94

"Loveliest Night of the Year" was approaching the million mark and would give him a distinction never accorded any other Red Seal artist, his second gold record. He was the only Red Seal artist on juke boxes throughout the country.

At the studio Lanza threw a party for the members of the cast and crew of *Because You're Mine*. It was reportedly the biggest shindig at any studio ever. He gave all his friends gold wrist watches with special engravings. Gate crashers received the same gift, which most of them promptly took to their jeweler to have engraved.

Everybody wanted to be known as a friend of Mario Lanza—everybody but the studio brass. Dore Schary had no patience with him. Lanza didn't give a damn. "I'll worry about him when I stop making money," he snorted.

12

On the set of *Because You're Mine* there were bad times and good times, and sometimes just plain funny incidents. One afternoon they were shooting an outdoor scene with Mario doing K.P. duty, peeling potatoes. His family was watching the scene being shot. Tony had Colleen in his arms and the director called for quiet as the scene was being shot. From out of nowhere came Colleen's tiny voice: "What is Daddy doing with those garbage cans?"

"Cut!" the director called unhappily. "What are we running here, a nursery school?" Tony was asked to take the children home and Lanza fell over laughing. Each take cost the studio several thousand dollars.

Lanza got a kick out of teaching Colleen to ride the pony he gave her as a gift. Colleen cried one day because her pony was lonely in the stable. Lanza shushed her tears with a gift of two more ponies to keep the first one company.

That was typical of the way the Lanzas spoiled their children. There were servants all over the house whose primary function was to see after the children. There was somebody to take them to their meals, pick up after them, dress them, and take their sass. Betty's orders were quite stringent when it came to the children. The servants were there to serve, not to mete out any discipline. Neither Betty nor Mario tried to keep them in line. One hot summer day the Irving Aaronsons and their daughter were among the guests at poolside. Aaronson was swimming near Colleen, who was sitting on the edge of the pool, and accidentally splashed her. She jumped up, stamped her feet, and spit in his face. In front of the shocked guests she screamed, "I'll have my Daddy fire you for that." Aaronson worked for MGM, not Mario Lanza, but to the Lanza children everybody worked for "Daddy."

Terry was embarrassed. "You can't go back into the pool until you apologize to Mr. Aaronson."

Betty, watching from the sidelines, interrupted when it looked as if Colleen was about to be taught a lesson. "Come on," she said, "it's not a federal case." Turning to Irving she laughed, "Look out for her. She's a tigress like her father." Terry felt she should have been given a good spanking; instead Betty treated the incident as something cute.

When Lanza rebelled against the studio he was as child-like and spoiled as his offspring. At one point during the filming of *Because You're Mine* he became upset with Dore Schary and went on a hunger strike. Terry was seriously worried. "Mario," he begged, "you can't do this to yourself. It's bad for your heart to be going up and down in your weight."

"Don't worry about me, Terry. I'll show the front office who they're dealing with." He refused to believe he was hurting himself instead of his enemies. Once he made up his mind, he was difficult to sway. His weight ranged from 180 to 240, and in the picture he appears almost to be two different men.

Offers for big concert tours were coming in from around the world. The offers agitated Lanza. "Look at all the money I'm losing. All I ever hear is how much money I spend. Well," he cried, "there it is out there—millions—and I'm stuck here trying to finish this lousy picture that I didn't even want to do in the first place."

The picture was finally completed, but it had been an unpleasant experience. For the first time Lanza had fought openly with Joe Pasternak. To show his contempt, after a very bad scene on the set one day, he had ordered Terry to drive him to Pasternak's house late at night. He got out of the car, took down his pants, and had a bowel movement on the lawn.

"Get me some leaves from those bushes," he said, "and I hope he's not growing poison oak as a hobby."

With the picture completed, Lanza felt great, knowing it was behind him. But controversy followed him around. Some of the city's prominent Italian-Americans were angry at him for refusing to appear at the Italian Flood Relief benefit which was being staged in Los Angeles.

He had sent a check to the Relief Fund and a note explaining why he couldn't appear. It did no good. His countrymen had been offended. The night of the event the master of ceremonies (Chef Milani) denounced Lanza from the stage. "He sings for a Jewish benefit (The Jewish Home for the Aged) and the Friars, but not for people of his own blood." The check that Lanza sent was never mentioned. The local Italian/American newspaper picked up the cudgel and went to work on Lanza.

By now Lanza was used to such criticism. It was offset by the high regard his fellow artists had for him and the accolades that continued to come his way.

One evening on his radio show he sang a song written by singer Frankie Laine in collaboration with his pianist Carl Fisher. The song was "When You're in Love." Both Laine and Fisher came to the studio to watch the program from the soundproof producer's booth. When it was over Laine rushed out, embraced Lanza, and said, "I never heard anything like it in my life."

It was not unusual for other stars to respond enthusiastically to a Lanza performance. He attracted other singers and musicians to his recording sessions and radio broadcasts. His magnetism captured everybody and a room lit up when he entered.

Interestingly both Helen O'Connell and Lanza recorded and enjoyed big hits of the same two songs, "The Loveliest Night of the Year" and "Wonder Why." "A good song," Lanza explained, "is a good song. Miss O'Connell is a fine singer. Good song, good singer—big hit."

Lanza never found fault with a fellow artist's work. He had too much respect for talent. Because of this, the attempts of gossip columnists to stir up a feud between Lanza and Kathryn Grayson fell especially flat.

Although Grayson and Lanza didn't agree on everything, they were good friends. They had little tiffs on the set from time to time, but that was normal. One evening Lanza had Terry drive him to Grayson's home. He climbed a tree beside the house, and from his position he could look into her bedroom window. "I want to see what she *really* looks like," he told Terry.

Grayson, with her window open, wasn't fooled for a second. "Mario, I know that's you out there. You're a naughty boy. Get down and go home or I'm going to call Betty and tell her how silly you are." Lanza sheepishly obeyed.

Lanza, along with Doris Day, was a recipient of the *Photoplay* Gold Medal Award for 1951. The award ceremony was held at the Ambassador Hotel. Every big name in the film industry was present. Studios bought up tables in blocks. After dinner when Lanza was presented with his gold medal, he said, "I am grateful to many people, but I want to especially thank three of them for contributing so much to my success." He singled out Frank Sinatra (who was stunned), Hedda Hopper (equally amazed), and Joe Pasternak, with whom he had had so much trouble on his last picture. Pasternak turned to Hopper and gasped, "This is a great thrill for me."

Lanza could not hold a grudge for long against a man whose skill and professional attitude he respected.

Having lost so much weight during the filming of *Because You're Mine*, Mario was recalled to the studio to reshoot a few scenes in order to blend the fat and thin of things into a better sequence of scenes. He never objected, reasoning that the studio was recognizing that he was an important star. He saw it as a victory over the studio hierarchy.

With Lanza the biggest star of the year, it was not surprising that MGM would come around to seeing things his way. The studio announced that his next film would be *The Student Prince*, a costume picture, the kind he had been begging for.

"Finally," he said happily, "they are beginning to recognize that there is more to me than fuss and feathers."

To celebrate, he went out on the day of the announcement and bought his parents a new home overlooking the Pacific. Mary and Tony moved in shortly afterward, with Terry. Lanza, who couldn't stay away from Mary's home-cooked Italian meals for long, was a frequent visitor.

It was after one of those meals, around Easter, that Betty said, "I have an announcement to make. I'm pregnant again." Lanza got up from his seat, went to her, and cuddled his wife in a big bear hug. "I'm so happy," he said. "Again in April. That means we'll have another December baby." He opened a bottle of champagne, and toasts were made.

It was a happy time for the Lanzas. Mario enjoyed his (or anybody's) children and would often get down on the floor to play games with them. It was difficult to tell who had the most fun, Lanza or the children. Kids of all ages loved him and he responded generously.

With a new baby coming he and Betty were looking for a bigger house for themselves. "I'd like to move into Bel Air, where they have the police patrol system," he said. "So let's look for a place."

He was getting ready to start prerecording for *The Student Prince*. Joe Pasternak would produce. Sonya Levien and William Ludwig (of *The Great Caruso*) would write the screenplay. Lanza made sure that there was additional music by his friends Nick Brodszky and Paul Francis Webster. He felt it would enhance the already famous Sigmund Romberg musical.

Never had he been more excited about a film. He wanted this picture to outdo even *The Great Caruso*.

*Private Antonio Cocozza,
U.S. Infantry—wounded in
Argonne Forest, France,
World War I—father of
Mario Lanza.*

*Maria Cocozza,
Mario Lanza's mother.*

Eight-year-old Freddie Cocozza when he made his First Communion in South Philadelphia.

Freddie Cocozza at sixteen, having fun with the girls in Wildwood, New Jersey.

Mario and Betty Lanza, married by a justice of the peace in Beverly Hills, California.

Lanza signs his MGM contract with studio boss, Louis B. Mayer.

Lanza's first major film, That Midnight Kiss, *in which he played a singing truck driver. (From the MGM release* That Midnight Kiss © *1949 Loew's Inc. Renewed 1976 by Metro-Goldwyn-Mayer Inc.)*

Lanza and his new singing partner, Gisele MacKenzie, chat between numbers during rehearsal for their Sunday evening CBS radio show for Coca-Cola. Gisele guested twice on "The Mario Lanza Show" and drew such enthusiastic comment that she was added permanently to the show. *(Photo by Eddie Hoff)*

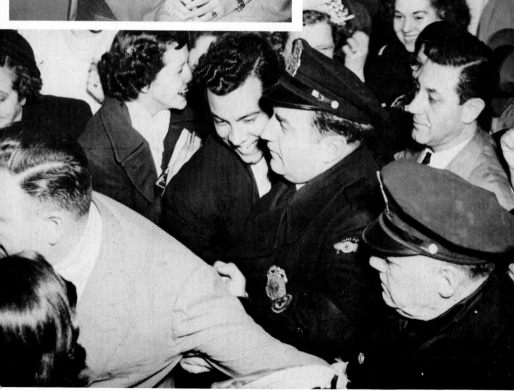

Even police had a tough time escorting Lanza through the crowds of fans when he returned to his home town following the opening of his first major film.

Lanza as Pepe Duval in The Toast of New Orleans
with Kathryn Grayson and David Niven. (From the
MGM release The Toast of New Orleans © *1950 Loew's Inc.*
Renewed 1977 by Metro-Goldwyn-Mayer Inc.)

Lanza with Mary and Tony and Ann Blyth during the filming of The Great Caruso, *the day Mary and Tony worked in the film.*

Terry Robinson with Lanza on the set of The Great Caruso. *Terry was Mario's stand-in for the picture.*

Dorothy Kirsten and Lanza in a scene from La Bohème *in* The Great Caruso. *(From the MGM release* The Great Caruso © *1951 Loew's Inc. Renewed 1977 by Metro-Goldwyn-Mayer Inc.)*

Because You're Mine *barracks fight between Lanza and James Whitmore. Terry Robinson, to the left of Mario, staged the scene. (From the MGM release* Because You're Mine © *1952 Loew's Inc. Renewed 1980 by Metro-Goldwyn-Mayer Inc.)*

*Lanza, Harry James, and Betty Grable in the
"Shower of Stars" TV Show.*

Lanza works out with his sparring partner
Terry Robinson in his gymnasium.

The Lanzas in a happy
moment celebrating their
wedding anniversary.

An overweight Lanza and his wife, Betty, arrive in Italy. It signaled the beginning of Lanza's comeback after being suspended by MGM and hit for back taxes by the IRS.

Lanza, Betty, and children, Ellisa, Damon, Marc, Colleen, in front of their palatial villa in Italy.

Lanza sings "Arrivederci Roma" in The Seven Hills
of Rome. *The little girl is an Italian street singer,
whom Mario heard and put in the film made in Italy.*

*Lanza meets the Queen of England after his
successful Command Performance.*

Zsa Zsa Gabor prepares to pour the champagne given her by Lanza to celebrate their first day on the set of For the First Time *in Rome.*

Betty and the children let Lanza have it in Zurich,
Switzerland, the family's first real vacation together.

Canio as played by Tonio Costa (Mario Lanza) sings "Vesti la giubba" from Pagliacci, *one of the great opera scenes in* For the First Time.

13

To save time and money the studio gave Lanza a soundproof room over the snack bar to rehearse his music for *The Student Prince.* On previous films studio business was bound to be interrupted whenever he rehearsed, because employees would gather around to listen to him.

For a while everything seemed fine. Lanza had been given the picture he wanted. He liked to share his good moods; one day when *Variety* ran a story about his mother's village in Italy, he rushed over to his parents' home to show them. The small town of Tocca Sasavria had asked the movie theatre in a neighboring city to depart from its tradition of showing only Italian films. They wanted to see *The Great Caruso.* Their request was granted and the day it was shown almost two hundred people from the village came by foot, bicycle, horseback, or buggy, carrying food, to have their first view of Mario Lanza on screen.

After eleven months *The Great Caruso* had grossed 19 million dollars.

From the inside, however, Terry saw that the excesses and pressures of the Lanzas' life were beginning to catch up with them. Both Mario and Betty were heading for nervous breakdowns. The first sign of disaster was the sudden departure of Sam Weiler. The break had been coming for some time as Mario and Sam grew farther apart. Nevertheless, when Sam left for "the Pocono Mountains to recuperate," as one columnist put it, Lanza was shaken. Weiler had been like a second father to him and Betty had depended on Sam for almost everything.

She immediately took to her bed and the doctor was summoned. How could she possibly run the house without Sam's help, she wanted to know. The doctor, seeing the distraught state she was in, told her to stay in bed and prescribed sedatives. "You know how difficult it is for her to carry a baby," he warned Lanza. "We don't want her to lose it."

There were other defections from the staff, including Jack Keller. Lanza, who tended to overreact emotionally to every little thing, fell into a depression. He became moody and suspicious of everybody, even Terry.

"He jumps at me now for nothing," Terry told Mary and Tony. "I suggested he start prerecording sessions for the picture to get the studio off his back. He only blew up. It's not like him."

The Lanzas moved into their new home in Bel Air and Terry and Mario's parents hoped things would start looking up.

Within three days the boys had an office set up for Mario. Two girls were put on salary to mail out fan photos, keep in touch with fan clubs around the world, and answer the bags of fan mail that were stacked about the rooms. The fans were loyal to Mario and apparently cared nothing about his squabbles with MGM.

Mario also had a music-room studio in the new house, plus a portable gymnasium for his boxing exercises. He never wanted for sparring partners because he always surrounded himself with ring veterans, having been an admirer of prize-fighters since his youth. He was proud of his new home and had real privacy for the first time. Still he did not return to the Mario of just a few months back. Something unusual had happened to him when the break with Sam came. He couldn't believe that such a thing could happen within his "family."

His behavior was now completely unpredictable: He would swing from one mood to another without warning. He finally agreed to go to a recording session that had been set up at Republic Studios for RCA Victor. In a pique, after an argument with Betty, he refused to keep the recording date and set RCA back 8,000 dollars. (They later deducted that amount from his royalties.)

Several days later he was in an "up mood" and decided to start on the songs for *The Student Prince*, so Terry drove him to MGM, where a sound stage was readied for him. He was quiet throughout the day except when actually singing. He recorded "Beloved," which had been written by Nick Brodszky and Paul Francis Webster, singing with great fervor, as if it were "tonight or never" for the girl of his dreams.

When he finished, he said to Terry, "Come with me to the men's room. I want to show you something."

The two men stood by the urinals and Lanza extended his penis and squeezed. There was an excretion of some sort. Terry panicked, "My God, you didn't get yourself a dose, did you?"

Lanza shook his head. "No. I had an orgasm when I sang. That's what a song can do for me. I put so much into the song that my entire body gives." He cleaned himself up and said, "Let's go listen to the playback."

After the song had been played back, director Curtis Bernhardt came over to Lanza and said, "I do not like the way you did that song. In this part, you are a Prussian prince and a Prussian soldier would sing with less emotion."

Lanza exploded. "That's why *they* never had any famous singers. What the hell's the difference what you are when you tell a girl it's tonight or never? You tell her from your soul. You tell her from your body. It's the last word. You wouldn't understand that. The song stays just as it is."

He was quiet the rest of the day but later went to Pasternak and asked him to fire Bernhardt. "I can't work with him. He has no sensitivity for good music." Pasternak said there was

103

nothing he could do. Bernhardt had a contract and the studio would honor it. Although Lanza continued to record his music, he avoided Bernhardt.

The day he recorded "I'll Walk with God" (also written by his friends Brodszky and Webster) he asked Terry to stop the car in front of the church in Beverly Hills that he and Betty attended. "I want to go in for a minute. Wait for me in the back." Terry watched as Lanza walked to the front of the church, where he knelt in front of the altar and prayed. When he returned he said "Okay, let's go to the studio—but keep people away from me. I want to be alone today."

He did the song in one take and walked away after the playback. Usually, he would discuss the recording with Pasternak or his conductor. This time he asked Terry to take him directly home.

"Get a good night's sleep," he said.

"You, too," Terry responded.

"I'll try," Lanza said, "but don't bet on it."

The first day of principal shooting was announced and when Lanza was driven to the studio he appeared to be in excellent spirits. As he was being made up, an assistant director, one who had worked on a previous film and caused a lot of trouble with the extras, came in and announced, "Mr. Lanza, you're wanted on the set in half an hour."

Without looking up from his makeup chair Lanza asked, "Is Curtis Bernhardt going to direct?"

"Yes," the assistant snapped; then he turned and disappeared. Lanza grew quiet. Several minutes passed and Terry reminded him they were waiting on the set.

"Get the car," Lanza said. "I want to go for a ride."

"Are you kidding? You have to go to the set. The whole crew is waiting."

"You want to go back to the set, then go. I'll take a ride by myself." Terry followed Mario's wishes. When the car went out through the studio gate the policeman on duty called the executive offices of MGM and within minutes everybody at

Metro knew that Lanza had fled the lot with an entire set waiting for his appearance.

"I don't want to go home, Terry. Let's go out to John Carroll's place in Chatsworth." Carroll, for years a handsome leading man at MGM, had his own differences with the studio and was sympathetic to Mario.

Carroll's would be his hideout for a few days until things settled down. Mario reasoned (but not very rationally) that the studio would see the error of their ways and that pressure would be brought by the cast and crew on Dore Schary, who would in turn get a new director. He didn't know or understand the will of Dore Schary.

Betty was sent for and joined Mario at Carroll's ranch. He explained to her why he had walked off the set. "They double-crossed me, so naturally I cannot do the picture." Lanza was feeling persecuted. He trusted no one, even hinting that Terry might be spying on him for MGM. "I want Bernhardt replaced, and that gopher assistant who was so insulting to me this morning." In his own mind, everybody was out to get him.

John Carroll was an expert talker and weaver of tales. He spoke of his own problems with Hollywood, and MGM in particular. It was the kind of conversation Mario wanted. The fact that somebody was on his side made him feel better.

Shortly afterward Mario, Betty, and Terry returned to the Bel Air house, where Lanza was apprised that MGM had suspended him. Not only was he off salary at the studio, but Dore Schary had exercised clauses in his contract which now prevented him from doing his Coca-Cola radio show. His income was suddenly reduced to record royalties. MGM became the big bad wolf with Lanza's millions of fans. How dare they take away his radio show. It had nothing to do with movies. Mario said Sam had allowed him to sign a bad contract.

"I cannot believe that Sam has so badly managed my

business affairs," he complained. "I was like a son to him."

Meanwhile, Lanza's agents at MCA were giving out press releases stating that only a technicality was holding up the picture, that Mario in fact loved the script and had a friendly feeling toward the studio. Lanza had his camp and MGM had theirs.

It was a standoff. Hoping to move the situation, Lanza called Terry into his bedroom one day and said, "They're calling me a lot of names. The world has fallen in on me. I'm a sick man. Sometimes I can't remember things. Lately I don't seem to connect on everything. But I think you could help me and do me a big favor. Get Mom and Pop and bring them to Metro. Let Schary and those guys meet my parents. Let them see the kind of stock I come from. Let them know I'm not one of their bums."

The studio agreed to see the elder Cocozzas. After all, they were in a dilemma themselves and were amenable to finding a solution. Mario was a valuable property. The studio had a lot of money invested in him and in the film. If the impasse could be broken, they didn't particularly object to bending a little by seeing his parents if that would make Lanza happy.

Terry picked up Mary and Tony and took them to the studio, and the three of them were ushered into Nick Schenck's office, where he was having lunch. They were joined by MGM executives Eddie Mannix, Benny Thau, Joe Pasternak, and Dore Schary, the studio chief.

Mary and Tony explained how unhappy Mario was over the breakup with his manager, his wife's prolonged illness, and a deluge of bad press, although they didn't express Lanza's feelings that MGM was responsible for most of the bad publicity.

"I understand," Schenck said. "I have children myself. There are often problems that must be worked out. I'll see that he gets a chance to rest once the picture is finished—if he wants to come back here and behave himself."

Terry spoke to Mannix. "Mario needs help now. You may not know it, but he's about to have a nervous breakdown. He's

106

not well. Can you do anything here at the studio to help alleviate his condition?"

"Mario is a big star," Mannix said. "He means a lot to this studio. We sympathize with him, but he's only one man. We have a big studio to run. No one man can jeopardize it. We must maintain discipline."

"But the man has problems. Mental problems. He needs help," Terry insisted.

Mannix was firm. "They all need help. How can we possibly give in to one man's temperament? It would disrupt the entire operation. You must understand one thing, Mr. Robinson. MGM is a factory. We turn out a product. We have a production line. The product comes first. Otherwise we would all be out of business."

He had not listened to a thing Terry said, or else had chosen to ignore or, worse, not believe him. Nothing was accomplished.

The Hollywood press, of course, was having a field day with Lanza's suspension. A long-standing interview was coming up with Jim Bacon, who covered Hollywood for the Associated Press, and on that morning Betty took ill. Mario refused to leave her bedside and wouldn't allow anyone to call a doctor. "I don't want to alarm anyone," he said. "I'll stay with her and let her get some rest. I want the house kept absolutely quiet."

"What about the interview with Jim Bacon?" Terry asked.

"Forget it. I'm in no mood for an interview. Call Jim and cancel it." Terry didn't cancel it. He reasoned it was too late to do that and was sure he could come up with a plausible excuse.

Terry was reading in the living room when the doorbell rang and Jim Bacon appeared, smiling and ready to conduct the interview.

Terry said, "Jim, I tried to reach you all morning to tell you that Mario had to go to a special meeting at MCA and asked that we set the interview for another time."

Jim, obviously disappointed, nevertheless said, "Okay. Call me when Mario comes back and we'll reset it."

He got into his car, and as he was pulling out of the driveway an unmistakable sound came bursting from the upstairs bathroom window. Lanza was singing in the shower. Jim Bacon stopped to enjoy the free concert. He wrote about it a few days later but in a good-natured manner, and he and Lanza remained friends.

Jimmy Fiddler, the Hollywood columnist and radio gossip, was not his friend and constantly attacked him. "Why should he be sent a warning," Fiddler wrote, "when as recently as four weeks ago he had reportedly cost the studio $5,000 by refusing to report for a recording session for which forty musicians, cameramen, and technicians had been assembled?"

Other papers picked up the cry. "His conduct has been irresponsible and frequently inexcusable," the *Journal American* said, but it went on to observe: "On the other hand, Mario at the request of his employers recently took off 75 pounds of weight in a short time. Anyone who has dieted strenuously can understand what a mental and physical ordeal this can be. Additionally he has lost practically all his savings through bad investments. All of this is enough to get an elephant down. Actors are humans, not machines." It was one of the few defenses he found in print.

Mary asked him at dinner one evening, "Fred, why don't you answer these people back who say such bad things about you? Why let them talk this way about you?"

He refused to defend himself in print. "Mom, don't worry. The truth will come out. I don't have to talk to anyone. Let them say what they want." Although he refused to answer his critics and pretended not to care, it dismayed him that the press could praise him when he brought a dying child to Hollywood and gave her some joy, and then attack the minute he disagreed with his studio or some Hollywood executive.

Though Lanza didn't know it, Dore Schary had been receiving almost daily reports of everything he did, both at the studio and in his private life—especially when he was away from his wife, out on the town. Before taking final action against him, Schary sent Lanza a telegram asking him to come to the studio. Richard Handley, who later left MGM to become Elizabeth Taylor's personal secretary, was Schary's secretary and admitted Lanza to Schary's inner office. Terry sat in the outer office with Handley, but the screaming and yelling could be heard in the outer chambers.

"I have a list here," Schary said, "of all your misdeeds. And look at you—you dress like a bum. MGM has a star image to maintain. You don't even look like a star." Schary went over the list of items that had been reported to him outlining Mario's bad conduct.

When Lanza left Schary's office, he was pale and trembling with anger. He said nothing until they were in the car on their way home. Then it all came out. He called Schary every name in the book and accused him of spying on him. "The guy used every bum he could find and had them get to me the only way they could—behind my back. People I've befriended. People I've helped."

Eventually his tirade subsided. He was tired, beaten, and heartsick. "I will not be doing *The Student Prince* now, so let's go home.

MGM's announcement on the matter was made in the form of a lawsuit. The studio sued for almost $700,000 in special damages, plus $4.5 million in general damages. The studio contended it would take that amount to cover their losses when the film was cancelled. They obtained an injunction preventing Lanza from appearing in concerts, singing on the radio, or making records for the duration of his current contract, which had fifteen months to go.

Lanza was closer to broke (for a star) than he realized. To make matters worse he discovered he owed the government back taxes.

Because You're Mine was previewed to mixed reviews. Lanza's talent deserved a better script.

"I told everybody I wanted to do a costume movie, not an Army comedy," he said. "They've made me look like a freak, a joke." Those around him assured him the picture was fine and the public would love it. He shook his head. "You're just being kind. I know the truth. I'll never go see it myself. Never!"

He was as surprised as anybody else when it was announced that *Because You're Mine* was selected by Queen Elizabeth of England for a Royal Command Performance. But he declined the Queen's invitation to attend. He sent a message to Her Majesty which said in part, "Since my wife is ill and we are expecting another baby, I won't be able to attend. I won't leave Betty in her condition."

The film was shown at London's Empire Theatre on Leicester Square on October 27, 1952. It was the first time a Hollywood musical had been chosen for this top event of Britain's movie year. Also, for the first time in memory, the star of a command show was not present. It was taken by much of the American and British press to be a snub to the queen. British papers asked a persistent question: Why had the trade committee of nine picked for a command performance one of the thinnest musicals of the year with little more to it than the excellent voice of Mario Lanza.

Lanza's reaction was predictable, considering his feelings about the film from the beginning. "Well, I guess when I complained to Pasternak, I was temperamental. Now the press is bearing out my feelings."

The film critics' consensus was that in spite of everything, the bad story, Mario's fights with MGM, and the lawsuits now pending, the picture would fare well for the studio and more than compensate them for any losses they might project for the apparently abandoned *The Student Prince*.

With Sam Weiler out of town, Mario, Terry and John Carroll raided the corporation offices, brought all of Mario's files to John's house and photographed each piece of paper. When Sam's attorney, Jerry Geisler, demanded return of the files, Mario did so gleefully. He had what he wanted.

Sam Weiler gave an interview to the Dallas *News* in which he stated that Lanza was not broke, that he was even with his taxes for 1951 and had a six-figure fortune in the bank. (Mario said he couldn't find any fortune.) As to the reasons for their break, Sam added, "I was becoming too emotionally involved. But I don't need Mario financially. I can buy and sell him ten times over."

That comment stung Lanza. "Sure he can buy and sell me; with *my* money. So my taxes are paid. How come I owe the government a quarter of a million dollars?"

Once again it was time for changes in the Lanza regime. New lawyers and business agents were hired.

Mario and Betty continued to ignore invitations. Colleen and Ellisa were the beneficiaries of their unsociable attitude toward the Hollywood community. They had Mommy and Daddy home all the time and Daddy could tell some pretty good stories. Most of Lanza's happiness came from his relationship with the two girls. He enjoyed telling them fairy tales. He created some rather ugly characters and then impersonated the voices. The youngsters giggled with fright and excitement. They loved their father and saw him as an anchor. Lanza above all else wanted to be a good father.

As if he didn't have enough trouble, Louella Parsons printed that Betty had a parking lot boy fired from a posh Beverly Hills store while Christmas shopping. Lanza called the store manager to ask him to give Parsons a different story for the boy's firing, but the columnist was right on target this time. Betty had indeed slapped the boy's face and insisted he be fired for "rudeness." She carried Lanza's celebrity status like a caveman with a big club. Betty knew who they were and she insisted that everybody respect that—or else!

Dore Schary suggested that Lanza check into Menninger's Clinic for psychiatric treatment. Lanza said he would talk to any nearby doctor MGM recommended, but he would not leave Betty, who was close to the birth of their third child.

It was arranged for him to see Dr. Augustus Rose at UCLA Medical Center.

Dr. Rose and Lanza hit it off immediately. The doctor was fond of opera and Mario enjoyed the long hours they talked together. But when he came home he complained, "See, I'm doing as the studio says, but how can anyone cure a broken heart? Can Dr. Rose change my life? Can Dore Schary remake me? With all this business involving Weiler and with Betty being so sick, the press jumping on me at every turn, what am I supposed to do? Take water and become a Boy Scout? If I did all those things expected of me then I wouldn't be singing and I wouldn't be fit to live with."

14

In December Betty gave birth to their first son, a baby weighing eight pounds, six ounces. It was the third December child for the Lanzas. The boy was named Damon Anthony, Damon because of Mario's admiration of writer Damon Runyon. Mario seemed to perk up. He finally had a son to carry on the Lanza name.

Lanza still refused to see outsiders. He wouldn't even see Lew Wasserman, his agent, who came by in a chauffeur-driven limousine with a royalty check.

"I don't care who it is. Just get the check," he advised the butler. He gladly accepted the $50,000 check but complained that Wasserman wasn't standing up for him against MGM and Dore Schary.

Although Lanza's only income was from record royalties, it was enough for him to afford the monthly rent on a lavish Palm Springs residence where he planned to sit out his fight with the studio. Lanza was too restless to sit around for long, though.

One day he was working out with Terry and said, "Let's disappear for a few days . . . drive up to Las Vegas and visit Ray Sinatra." (Sinatra was now working as an orchestra leader at one of the hotels there.)

Terry said what he always said when Lanza wanted to go someplace—yes.

"Go to the bank and get me $1000 in singles and have them put wrappers around them in $50 bundles." Terry obliged.

Lanza had a small pirate's treasure chest that had come as a gift filled with candies. He lined the bottom with paper and then placed the bundled money on top, giving the impression that the chest was full of cash.

On the way to Las Vegas they stopped for gasoline in the desert. The young Mexican boy who was handling the pump recognized Lanza. "Hey, you are the movie picture fella. I see you kiss all those girls. Boy, you okay. You can sing, too." Lanza rewarded the boy's enthusiasm with one of the fifty dollar packets and he and Terry drove off, leaving the kid in amazement.

Lanza created a sensation among the bellboys at the Sands Hotel, dispensing his fifty-dollar packets as tips. After three days of resting and shopping for gifts (he did not gamble) they returned to Palm Springs.

A week later he took ill and a doctor was called in. After an examination the doctor informed him, "You must be careful. You are a bit on the diabetic side." Grandpa Lanza suffered from diabetes and Lanza shuddered at the thought of insulin shots: he hated needles no matter how small.

A week later he had his first attack of gout. He awakened at three in the morning, his big toe enormously swollen and the pain excruciating. He was confined to his bedroom for several days. His excesses were beginning to take a physical toll.

Terry took on a new job—that of Lanza's press representative. One of his first duties was to announce that Lanza had met with Eddie Mannix at MGM and that things were looking up. After the meeting Lanza seemed more cheerful and began to work out with Mickey Golden and a couple of other boxers, making use of the ring which had been set up on the patio.

Without fanfare, MGM dropped its lawsuit against Lanza and it appeared he would be returning to do *The Student Prince*. The press applauded his "change of attitude" and MGM's "benevolent feeling for a member of the Metro 'family.' "

The truce didn't last. On April 11, 1953, the papers bannerlined the story: "Mario Lanza Fired by MGM." Dore Schary's statement was brief: "Lanza has been shown every consideration. Over the months *The Student Prince* has been scheduled and rescheduled at an increasing financial loss. . . . His latest demands on the studio are unacceptable."

Lanza claimed he had been double-crossed. "I notified the studio last week by letter that I would report to them at the time specified." He quoted from the letter. "Will you please advise me to whom, what hour and date you desire me to report." MGM ignored his claim. Through *Box Office* magazine, MGM announced that *The Student Prince* would be made without Lanza. Rather than admit the studio had defeated him, Lanza shrugged his shoulders and said, "Every studio in town wants me for a picture. If I accept everything I'm offered I'll make $3 million this year."

The real reason for his meeting with Eddie Mannix came to light after his dismissal. In return for the dropping of the lawsuit, Lanza had agreed to allow the studio the right to use his recordings of the score for the film. At MGM's request he even came back on the lot for one day to rerecord "Beloved," the song that director Curtis Bernhardt considered too sexy. The number was done in one take, and once the news got around that Lanza was on the lot, workers deserted other sets to come and see him. It was obvious that Lanza's firing was strictly an executive decision.

The truth was, Lanza was in no physical or mental condition to begin a heavy costume picture like *The Student Prince.*

The MGM executives were aware of his dilemma and many Hollywood watchers felt that Dore Schary was being vindictive by not allowing him a greater say in choosing the film's director and starting date. More than a few people in the industry have blamed Schary for the talent and financial problems that beset MGM following Louis B. Mayer's exit as studio head. The truth was that Hollywood had fallen on hard times because of the advent of television, and Schary was faced with a difficult situation. Both he and Lanza were victims of the collapse of the studio system. In the old days, stars did as they were told. Now they wanted complete control over their careers. This doesn't seem unreasonable today in the era of superstars. But the studio system had functioned as a not always benevolent dictatorship. That the demands of the stars should occur at a time of economic instability in the industry was bound to result in battles and defections. Lanza was not the only star having troubles with his studio.

MGM announced that British actor Edmund Purdom would play the leading role in *The Student Prince*, mouthing Lanza's singing. When the film was released, reaction to Purdom would be unenthusiastic. In fairness to Purdom, the public probably would have rejected anybody in the role except Lanza. Lanza would delight in the debate, buying every paper and magazine that had anything in it about the movie or its new star, chortling with glee over every line.

With the MGM lawsuit dropped, Lanza had Terry drive him to the studio late one evening to clean out his apartment. Tony, the cop at the gate, knew him and let his car pass. After loading the car, they took a stroll through the lot. Lanza spotted Judy Garland, alone and tipsy, emerging from a screening room. He said hello and asked if he could give her a lift.

She said, "Sure." Lanza got in the back seat with Garland and told Terry to stop by a liquor store and pick up some Chivas Regal. For a while they sat in the car, drinking scotch from paper cups and dissecting the MGM executives whom they both detested. It made them happy. Garland had her head on Lanza's shoulder.

Suddenly Lanza said, "Terry, drive up to the Hollywood hills. It's quiet up there." Terry complied. Once there he got out of the car and took a walk. After a while, he went back to the car. The windows were fogged somewhat but he could see into the back seat. Lanza was on top of Garland, her legs up in the air. They were both yelling encouragement to each other. Terry beat a hasty retreat and waited for the noise to quiet down. When he got back in the car, Lanza said, "Let's take Judy home."

The following day Terry mentioned the incident to Lanza. "Suppose the cops had found you two in the car last night?"

Lanza said, "They would have gotten a kick out of meeting Judy and me. We may do a film together some day. We talked about it last night. She's the greatest woman singer around."

Lanza was now able to make records again and to accept other picture offers and concert dates. He immediately started to prepare for major recording sessions for RCA Victor and both he and Costa were busy working on arrangements and new songs. Costa wrote a song, "You Are My Love," which Lanza recorded in the first batch of new releases. RCA was not high on the song, but Lanza talked them into doing it. "Let's make the Greek a composer," he told the RCA executives, and they went along with him. During this same session he recorded, "Song of India," "If You Were Mine," and "Call Me Fool."

The RCA Victor executives in New York were anxious to rush out an album of songs from *The Student Prince*. They felt certain Lanza's popularity would carry the album but had doubts about how the public would react to someone else mouthing his songs on the screen. Would that hurt Lanza's record sales? The decision was that it would not, especially if the album was recorded and distributed as soon as possible.

Manny Sachs came out from New York to supervise the cutting of the album, which went on to sell over one million copies, in spite of Lanza's absence from the picture.

In the midst of these activities, Damon Anthony Lanza was baptized by Father Paul Maloney, who had also christened Lanza's two daughters. His godparents were Rose and Fred Gallachio, close family friends from Philadelphia.

In a buoyant mood after the christening, Lanza invited Adela Rogers St. John to his home to interview him. During the interview, she caught a glimpse of how indulgent the Lanzas were with their children. Ellisa came into the room, walked up to her father, and said, "Papa, sing to me." Lanza stared down at her but did not sing. Ellisa, hands on hips, tossed her head back demandingly. "Now, Mario, don't make me angry!"

Lanza thought her performance a delight and immediately burst into song.

The unpleasant business with Sam Weiler had to be resolved. Reluctantly, Lanza filed suit against his former manager for a little more than $250,000, accusing Weiler of fraud and negligence and demanding an accounting of all the money he had handled. Along with the lawsuit, he gave out a piece of information that must have been hard to swallow at Metro. Through his attorney, Robert Kopp, he said that he had merely wanted to shut off his huge income until he found a way to drop Sam Weiler from his personal payroll. It was not, Kopp contended, temperament on the part of Lanza that caused him to stall production of *The Student Prince*. It was Weiler all along.

Betty had a piece of news herself. "I'm pregnant again," she told Lanza, "and for once it looks like it's going to be a summer child." Soon afterward she took to her bed in anticipation of the usual nine-month ordeal.

Lanza was troubled. "This is the last baby you'll have," he said. "I don't want to see you so sick anymore."

It was during this pregnancy, however, that Lanza and Betty had one of their most violent fights. It was a tough pregnancy and she was often in a foul mood. Lanza was up to his ears in all kinds of problems. So it was no surprise to Terry one day when a maid came running into the den where he was reading the trade papers. "Come quick," she cried. "Mr. and Mrs. Lanza are fighting and he may hit her."

Terry rushed upstairs to their bedroom and jumped between them, pulling Lanza away. Betty was hysterical, calling her husband every dirty name she could think of. Terry urged her to get out of the room. As he spoke, Lanza, half-drunk, grabbed him around the throat in a half nelson and began to choke him. They wrestled to the floor. Instead of leaving the room, Betty took off her shoe and began hitting Terry on the head, screaming, "Leave Mario alone! You'll hurt him!"

Terry threw his arms up to protect himself. "Hey, I'm trying to help you. Stop hitting me."

Lanza sobered up fast. "Hey Betsy," he roared, "leave Terry alone. He just saved your life."

The tension broke and everybody laughed. It was just another day at the Lanzas.

With a new baby expected Mario and Betty once again decided they needed a larger house and they moved back to Beverly Hills. Lanza's new back yard overlooked the golf course of the Los Angeles Country Club, an exclusive club that discouraged the membership of actors.

Lanza did not like the rules of the club. He had an excellent view of the golf course from his music room and devised a gimmick to irritate club members as they made the rounds. He had a microphone and amplifier which he used to record practice tapes. When he saw a member raise his club to swing at the ball, he would let go with an amplified Lanza high note, completely distracting the perplexed golfer.

Lanza said good-bye to 1953 and started the new year on a much sourer note. The landlord of the house he had just moved out of sued him for $17,000. The owners listed missing items, held Lanza responsible for an illegally erected eight-foot fence across the front of the property and installation of exterior wiring without the owner's permission. The list of complaints was long and detailed. The suit was settled out of court but nevertheless got a big play in the papers.

More important, Lanza was hit with a claim from the Internal Revenue Service for back taxes amounting to $200,000. Lanza's reaction was typically emotional. He resumed his excessive drinking and would sit for days staring out the window. He refused to see or talk to anyone, even on the telephone. His professional staff had to be reduced; there

119

wasn't enough money to cover the tremendous overhead. Costa left to go on tour with another artist, and Maestro and Helen Spadoni volunteered to fill in and help Lanza with his music and with Betty. Mickey Golden went to work for actor Rory Calhoun. The government had put a lien on Lanza's record royalties and placed him and Betty on a strict budget. It was a blow to Lanza's ego as well as his purse.

One day he said to Terry, "Let's go for a drive. I want to get out of this place before I go crazy." He insisted that he drive, which surprised Terry because Mario never wanted to drive if he had someone to drive him. Terry moved over and Lanza slid in behind the wheel and they drove for a long time before Lanza broke the silence. His breathing and speech were affected by the 40 or 50 extra pounds he had allowed himself to put on through overindulgence and laziness. "I've lived a hundred years already. People have picked on me since I first came to this rotten town and now the government has moved in for the kill. What's the difference now? Life is over for me."

Lanza sounded mean and Terry had never before seen him in such a mood. He lapsed into silence and continued to drive away from the city along one of the narrow canyons that connected Beverly Hills with the San Fernando Valley. As the car climbed through the treacherous open chasm, Lanza increased his speed. The speedometer read 80 miles an hour and Terry cautioned him: "Hey, Tiger, you're going pretty fast. Don't you think you ought to slow up with all these curves?"

Lanza shrugged. "So what? What's life? A lot of crap. Suppose you were in my shoes. What the hell would you do? Everyone is out to get me. All my life I've tried to give and look where the hell I wind up. Alone with you in a car." Lanza was starting to cry.

Rather than upset him, Terry swallowed his fear and, placing both feet tightly against the floorboards, watched the speedometer climb to 90.

Oblivious to everything except his own feelings, Lanza went on. "Think of this. If I drive off this mountain, you and I would die in a burst of flames and every damn newspaper in the world would headline: Mario Lanza and best friend die in a flaming wreck. What an end for a tiger and a terror."

Terry began to pray silently, certain that Lanza had a death wish that he was about to fulfill. At the top of the hill Lanza slowed the car. He pulled over to the side of the road and wiped his eyes. They sat in silence for a time, and then he turned to Terry and said, "I'm sorry. Here, you drive."

They drove back to Beverly Hills, and as they approached the house, the front left tire blew out. "Just imagine if this tire had blown out when you were speeding," Terry said. "God didn't want you to die, Mario. You've got to reorganize your life. You're still the best talent in the world and you have your youth."

"Okay, preacher," he said. "Just don't tell Betty what happened today. She has enough problems without any help from me."

15

Betty had begun to suffer from convulsions and after a particularly severe one she was taken by emergency ambulance to a hospital, where she nearly lost the baby. The family doctor was questioned about it by Terry, who believed it was due to the uppers and downers that had been prescribed for her. The doctor indignantly advised him to mind his own business. Lanza, who was impressed by academic degrees and formal education, merely shrugged. "He's got a good European education. Betty swears by him. He must be okay."

Betty's doctor bills were large as were those of Mary, who was constantly in and out of the hospital. There wasn't enough money to pay for everything. The delivery men who used to stop in the kitchen for a cup of coffee with Lanza now waited outside and requested cash in advance before leaving groceries.

George London, on a rare visit to Hollywood, came to see Lanza and was shocked. In an aside to Terry he said, "My God, it's years since I've seen them but they're not the same people. Not just older. Something's happened. I'm frightened."

"The only help will have to come from within themselves," Terry said. "They don't seem ready to admit anything is wrong."

He hoped George would be able to stay awhile and be company for Lanza, but London was readying a concert tour for Europe and would be in town for only a few days. While he was there, Lanza perked up and they recalled old times when both were novices. The conversation always got around to *The Student Prince* which was soon to be released. Both agreed that the public wouldn't go for Lanza's voice coming out of Edmund Purdom's mouth.

Just to get out of the house, Mario accepted George's invitation to come and listen to him work with a new voice teacher. The Maestro had a music room behind his home. An older man, Mario couldn't help notice immediately that his wife was twenty-five years his junior. While George sang, Terry watched Mario slip out and into the back door of the Maestro's home. After a few minutes, Terry went looking for Mario. He found him in the kitchen corner having sex with the teacher's wife, her dress pulled up to her waist and backed against the wall. Terry slipped back to the music room. In time Mario joined him and applauded when George finished a song.

Driving back to the Lanza house afterward, George said, "The guy's not that good. They have better coaches in New York."

Mario laughed. "His wife's good though. She handled my high C with no difficulty."

George shook his head. "You'll never change."

Mario said, "You ought to try it, George. You'll sing better."

After George left, Lanza lapsed back into the melancholy state which had overtaken him when the Internal Revenue had lowered the boom. He had made so much money in his life that the thought of curtailing expenses was unbearable.

A more practical Betty sent her mink coat to Al Teitlebaum, Beverly Hills' most prestigious furrier on swank Rodeo Drive. She asked Terry to obtain as large a loan as possible on the expensive fur.

Teitlebaum, a longtime family acquaintance, was surprised. "I heard that Betty and Mario were in trouble, but I never realized it was *this* bad."

Terry leveled with him. "Since Mario split with Sam, everything has been downhill. He doesn't trust people anymore. He needs help from somebody like you." He got to the

123

point. "What I'm asking is, why don't you come over to the house and talk to Mario?"

Teitlebaum felt that it would be an intrusion and that Lanza might be insulted. "If they invite me, I'll come. Otherwise I don't think it would be wise."

Terry brought it up with Lanza, and Mario invited Teitlebaum over to discuss his growing financial problems. The result was that, on a handshake, the furrier became his new manager. Teitlebaum, a successful businessman, immediately made contacts with the other major studios to let producers know that Lanza was ready to work again.

On May 19, after a difficult labor for Betty, the Lanzas' fourth and final child, Marc, was born. With Mario's typical desire to bring business associates into his family, the Lanzas asked Al and Sylvia Teitlebaum to be the child's godparents.

Howard Hughes, through attorney Greg Bautzer, expressed an interest in starring Lanza in a new project. With typical eccentricity he asked Lanza to meet with him at an out-of-the-way photography shop on Melrose Avenue in West Hollywood at three o'clock in the morning. He was to park in the back alley, knock on the door, and wait.

At precisely 3:00 A.M. Terry knocked on the back door; Lanza chose to wait in the car. A tall man—not Hughes—emerged from the shadows and asked, "Where is Mario Lanza?" Terry motioned to the Cadillac behind him. "Tell him to come in," the half-hidden figure said. "You wait out here."

Lanza went inside for his meeting with Hughes, and Terry fell asleep in the car. Three hours later Lanza emerged. He shook Terry and said, "Wake up. Let's go."

As they drove home Lanza was enthusiastic. "My God, that man can talk forever. Still, I liked him. He wants to do a big musical in Texas. I hope we can work together."

The big musical never materialized and Lanza never heard from Hughes again. It became clear that Hughes, a Lanza fan, had simply wanted to spend some time with him.

Today's famous people are more rawly exposed to the public. During Mario's career they were not. Family life was dictated to the media via studio publicity releases. Celebrities, not unlike high strung race horses, are usually nervous and jittery and seldom ready for crisis. Mario's career was pockmarked by crisis. If it involved one of his children, it became an immediate red alert.

One evening after dinner, the children were playing hide and seek. From the den, where they were watching television, Mario, Betty, and Terry, suddenly startled by a child's anguished scream, jumped up almost in unison and ran to the source of the problem. Colleen had her finger caught in the crack of a swinging door. Damon had run through the doorway just as she stuck her finger in the door jamb. The tip of her finger was severed and blood was splattered everywhere.

Mario, who paled at the sight of blood, got down on his hands and knees and scoured the floor until he found the tip of Colleen's finger. At the emergency hospital an unsuccessful attempt was made to resuture the severed tip to the finger. Colleen was given an injection for pain and sent home to bed. Betty collapsed, was sedated and spent the next two weeks in bed. Mario found a bottle and spent the night by his daughter's bed, alternately crying and drinking.

The following day on Mario's orders all swinging doors in the house were removed and strict orders given to the help about the children's safety. Mario was fanatical about the safety of his offspring.

Work finally came Lanza's way when he was asked to co-star with Harry James and Betty Grable in a television special, "The Shower of Stars," to be aired on September 30 in prime time. Lanza, like most major stars of the period, had stayed away from the new medium. His fee for the show was $40,000 plus two new Chrysler cars, a gift from the sponsor.

A little heavy from so much inactivity, he went into training to get in shape for the show. He was aware of television's impact on the country. It would reveal him to millions of people instantly. He felt both a challenge and a certain anxiety.

Betty at this point was confined to her room. Whereas in the past she had given him advice, she now did nothing more than answer a few fan letters and see the children when they were brought in. Without her husband's knowledge she was also seeing her old masseuse who dispensed amphetamines and barbiturates on demand. The doctor, meanwhile, kept assuring Lanza that his wife was "just a little bit anemic."

The industry waited along with the public. Would Mario make a comeback or would he fall on his face once and for all, as so many of his critics anticipated. Many doubted he would ever work again. Taking off weight so rapidly made Lanza nervous and suspicious. He wouldn't do publicity for the appearance, didn't want to see the press, and in general created more controversy than was necessary.

Prior to the show he moved out of his bedroom and slept in his music room. Orders were given not to disturb him.

Terry offered to go home, but Lanza said, "No, stay with me. Sleep on the couch. You can answer the phone and keep people away." He adhered to a strict diet—a grapefruit for breakfast, one hard-boiled egg with coffee (no sugar) for lunch, and some fresh shrimp for dinner—and shed pounds daily.

But he was increasingly worried about reaction from the press. Terry tried to reassure him. "That's easy for you to say," Lanza argued. "Will they look at me and see a human being? No! They will say Lanza is fat. Lanza sings off key. Lanza overemotes. Lanza strains his high notes."

After a few days of listening to his complaints, Terry couldn't take it any longer and left to look after the health club he had recently opened in Beverly Hills. He was in the gym when Ace Alagna, publisher of the New Jersey *Italian Tribune*, came in with heavyweight champion Rocky Marciano. Lanza idolized Marciano, and Rocky, it turned out, was a Lanza fan. Terry and Ace brought the champ to Mario's house.

Terry rapped on the door of the music room. "Mario, it's me. I've got to see you."

They heard the door being unlatched and Terry shoved Marciano in front of him and stepped back. Lanza opened the door and said, "I told you I didn't want to be . . . my God, Rocky Marciano!"

The two burly Italians fell into each other's arms, hugging and kissing like long-lost brothers.

The lift Lanza got from Marciano's visit was temporary. Three days before the show was to air he developed a case of red throat and couldn't shake it. By then he had worked himself into such a state of anxiety over the television appearance that Terry couldn't be sure if the ailment was mental or physical.

Since he couldn't sing, CBS arranged for him to lip-synch some of his earlier recordings. His old buddy Jim Bacon caught on immediately and broke the story that "some two-year-old records were rushed over from his house for this spectacle."

CBS issued a denial. The show's director swore that Lanza had prerecorded the songs a day or so before the show, but Bacon was right and everybody in the music world knew it. The press went after Lanza. Sheilah Graham, who had become increasingly nasty, said, "Mario collects 40 G's pay without a song."

Chrysler was embarrassed, as was CBS. Yet the Trendex ratings showed the musical show had cornered 46.3 percent of the viewing audience, which was excellent. Nevertheless Lanza felt he had to do something to shore up his reputation. He told Terry to call a press conference. "I'll sing for the whole goddamn bunch—and this time no big meals for the freeloaders. Coffee and Danish will do. Walk them to my music room the long way when they get here; show them the grounds. Let them know I'm not washed up."

Terry obliged and the assembled journalists got a long tour from the front door to Lanza's music room. Spadoni was seated at the piano when they entered. He had once been with

Caruso and now looked especially dignified with his shock of white hair, French beret, and neatly trimmed and waxed mustache.

After the press were seated, Lanza kidded them a little and then said, "I'm going to sing opera because there's nothing phony about it." He looked directly at one newsman who had been particularly caustic in his review of the TV special. "With opera one can't lie or croon his way out of a bad situation."

When the free concert was over the critics went away convinced the mistake had been theirs, not Lanza's. Chrysler and CBS were delighted and Mario was brought back for another show, at the same salary and bonus—$40,000 and two new Chryslers. What was more important to him, Max de Schanensee, one of the top opera critics in the world, wrote a rave review of his performance. The review he clipped and pasted into his scrapbook. The automobiles he gave away to business associates.

Lanza was now officially back to work. Al Teitlebaum negotiated a deal with Warner Brothers for him to return to the screen. The vehicle was a film adaptation of James M. Cain's book *Serenade*. In addition to salary, Lanza would get 35 percent of the film's gross receipts. In spite of his troubles, the year was ending on a high note. He closed out 1954 with his usual Christmas soiree and a renegotiated three-year contract with RCA Victor.

The IRS, thanks to an arrangement with RCA agreed to release its lien against his income. To the Lanzas it meant they were back in business and out of bondage. The New Frontier Hotel in Las Vegas signed Mario for a $50,000 a week engagement for two weeks in April in their main room.

With fortune once more smiling on him, he and Betty put everything in storage, took the kids, and moved into the Palm Springs house to prepare for the engagement.

Away from Beverly Hills Lanza was more relaxed. Ray Sinatra joined them later to begin rehearsals and Andy and

Della Russell were frequent weekend visitors. Brodszky materialized and began writing music for *Serenade*.

A happy Lanza was full of energy and fun to be around. He was as normal as he would ever be. There were long walks with the family, tennis, swimming, boxing, and weightlifting. During the evenings the four children were gathered about the fireplace, where they were told hair-raising stories with sound effects (from Mario) and then bundled off to bed. Lanza accompanied them and sang them to sleep. Occasionally he and Betty took in a film at the local drive-in.

Lanza's case against Sam Weiler was settled out of court. "Give him whatever he wants. Make a settlement," Lanza ordered his attorneys. "Betty is in no mental state to fight Sam in court. She loves him like a father, and so do I. Anyway, why bring all this mess into court and have the world read it? I want my private life private." No longer on the brink of financial disaster, he saw no reason to go after Weiler. For the moment the future once more seemed secure.

A friend, screenwriter Ben Hecht, came down to Palm Springs for a visit one day and it stretched into a week. He was anxious to write an original story which would star Mario and would be produced by J. Arthur Rank in England. However, nothing ever came of it.

Betty, still leaning on pills to conquer her depression, got into a lengthy discussion about her condition with Mr. Hecht one evening. He assured her he knew just the right tonic for her problems. "As a matter of fact," he assured her "I am currently taking it myself. It works miracles." His miracle liquid was liquid chloral hydrate. He even ordered a bottle from his own pharmacist and presented it to her.

After a few days' use Betty was convinced she had never felt better in her life. She found a pharmacist who wrote her a blank prescription and she used it to keep herself supplied with the narcotic—quickly developing a dependency on it. It didn't take long for the convulsions to return. The alcohol and drug combination devastated her system and she was immediately hospitalized. After her release the chloral hydrate was replaced by Butisol. One crutch replaced another.

Terry preceded Lanza to Las Vegas to set up a press conference. It was the largest ever to be held there. Lanza arrived at the railroad station with a full entourage including his own personal hairdresser.

Las Vegas was cold and windy and the members of the press unruly. Cameramen pushed and shoved for position, frightening the children. Marc, the baby, started to scream, but the photographers insisted on a "family" shot and little Marc was not allowed to be taken away by his nurse until that had been accomplished. After an hour of popping flash bulbs, blustery weather, and strained tempers, the family was driven to the hotel to face another siege by ill-mannered press and photographers.

The final straw came when Betty saw how small their quarters were. "Is this where they're putting us? We're nine people!" When she was informed that their party had arrived earlier than expected and that the hotel was booked solid, she hit the ceiling. She called Al Teitlebaum in Los Angeles and he promised to come up the following day and straighten things out. In the meantime it was chaotic. Lanza and Betty slept with the baby. The rest made do with couches and folding beds.

One of the children had a cold and after a sleepless night everyone was coming down with a cold. Someone was sent out to the local Sears store to buy warm coats for the children. Ray Sinatra, now a Las Vegas resident, offered to take the children to his house but Colleen stamped her feet and said "No! We want to stay with Mommy and Daddy." In spite of the inconvenience, the children had their way.

Lanza, as usual, took the hotel's failure as a personal affront. He could not be objective about such occurrences. When he felt he had been wronged, he acted without thinking and tended to court disaster. Las Vegas is an important town for entertainers; this engagement could have meant a lot to Mario's career. But now, as if unconsciously fearing failure and not wanting to face the possibility, he became unco-operative. He refused to go to rehearsals and stayed in his room until the day of his scheduled opening.

That morning the Las Vegas papers carried full-page spreads hailing the opening as the biggest in the town's history.

Jack Entratter, who ran The Sands Hotel, was betting 3 to 1 that Lanza wouldn't show. He knew, because Mario spent the day at his hotel in the company of Ben Hecht and a bevy of show girls; he was "treating" a convenient attack of red throat with champagne. Al Teitlebaum arrived and, upon learning where his client was, went directly to The Sands and brought Lanza back to The Frontier. He could still make his opening if he would get a little rest and sober up.

"Call it off tonight," Lanza said, slurring his words. "I won't risk my voice for any amount of money."

The only way to cover up was to call in a doctor and have him issue a statement that Lanza was indeed ill.

The casino was packed with celebrities and press. The hotel was to have an open house—but there would be no Mario Lanza.

Betty, as usual during a crisis, came down with a fever. Mario took some sleeping pills and joined her in bed. Celebrities visited their suite but he would see none of them.

Jimmy Durante, appearing before the packed house that night, made the announcement: "Mario Lanza will be unable to sing for you tonight. He is a very sick boy and is under an oxygen tent."

Not many believed Durante's fib. Boos and laughter filled the place. Reporters rushed for telephones while Durante, Ray Bolger, Mindy Carson, and Frankie Laine put on a show for the audience.

The press once again pounced on Lanza. The consensus was that he had lost his nerve. The following day the hotel

131

cancelled his contract. He would be replaced by singer Billy Daniels. A spokesman for the hotel made the official announcement: "We don't know whether we're going to sue Lanza for this matter, but we don't think so. We feel very sorry for the man. We have no feeling he should be hurt any more than he already is." Lanza was washed up as far as Las Vegas was concerned.

Reporters met Lanza's train when it arrived back in Los Angeles. Asked if he felt guilty for not fulfilling his commitment at The Frontier, Mario said, "If I had any feeling of guilt toward myself, it would be like feeling guilty against God!"

Louella Parsons' account of the Vegas event was printed in the Sunday Los Angeles *Examiner*. She accused him of being afraid, with a fear that might silence his voice forever. "I am the only reporter," she said, "who saw Mario in Las Vegas and I saw him twice. . . . He looked like a million dollars, very thin, handsome, and fit. But when he opened his mouth to tell us about his sore throat, I knew the jig was up and that he would not sing at his widely advertised nightclub debut." She hinted that Lanza was again in debt and facing financial troubles.

Jack Warner didn't seem to think so. He made his own announcement: "We are going ahead with *Serenade*, as planned."

No sooner was Lanza settled in the new home that Al Teitlebaum had found for him than he began to feel restless. He and Terry took a drive to Tijuana, Mexico, along the scenic Pacific Coast Highway. Lanza put on dark glasses and a felt hat and wasn't recognized at the border crossing. After parking the car in a gas station, the two men got out and walked through the streets of Tijuana, turning away the street peddlers who tried to sell them everything from tacos to twelve-year-old virgin sisters.

They came to a cantina and Lanza suggested they stop for lunch. Inside there was a bar and some tables around a sawdust dance floor. The two men found a table in a dark corner of the room, away from the other customers.

As they sat over a lunch of enchiladas, tacos, and beer, a young Mexican, poorly dressed with a guitar strung across his shoulder, entered. He sat at the bar and ordered a beer and began to pick out a melody. Lanza listened for a while, then nudged Terry. "There's a real musician. He's never had a lesson and listen to the sound his fingers make."

The young guitarist drank his beer and started to play again. The tune was "Granada." Lanza hummed along, then without warning burst into song. He took the glasses off, the hat fell to the floor, and he continued to sing. The Mexican came closer and let out a cry: "Mario Lanza!"

The bartender, mindful of his business, ran into the streets yelling, "Lanza! Lanza! Lanza!"

Within seconds the place was jammed with people. Lanza, forgetting his desire for anonymity, stood up on the table and sang for more than half an hour. Old women came forward and kissed his hands. They spoke to him adoringly in Spanish and he answered in Italian.

He tapped Terry on the shoulder. "How much money are you carrying?"

"About $300."

"Let me have it."

He took the sum from Terry and handed it to the guitarist. By then the crowd was so large that the police were needed to help him out of the corner he was backed into. With a dozen policemen leading the way, he and Terry finally escaped. Lanza left his hat and glasses and even forgot to pay for their meal.

Terry couldn't understand it. Two weeks ago Lanza could have sung in Las Vegas for $100,000. Today he had performed for nothing and given away $300 for the privilege. Why?

Mario explained, "Even for all the money in the world I wouldn't jeopardize my voice. The people I sang for today are my people. They don't pick on me. They love me fat or skinny. They feel what I feel."

Terry had his doubts. He knew that the Mexico scene was

133

the easy part of the question; it was just Mario showing off and having a good time. He had met enough actors and entertainers to know that, as well as being sometimes brilliant and often dedicated artists, they were also compulsive performers and always "on." But what had happened in Las Vegas was more troubling. If Lanza could throw away an opportunity like that, there was no telling what he might throw away next.

16

The prerecording sessions for *Serenade* began encouragingly. Lanza walked into the recording studio with his musical director, Ray Heindorf, and completed his chores for the day in ten minutes. "It is the first time of my many years experience as the head of Warners' music department that any singing star has been letter perfect on one take," said Heindorf. The studios had been engaged for a full day. Lanza was in and out in less than fifteen minutes.

The rest of the sessions went equally well. There were selections from operas, and Nick Brodszky wrote two songs for the film, "Serenade" and "My Destiny."

Lanza was his old playful self. At MGM he had amused himself by chasing Joe Pasternak's secretary around her desk and giving her a squeeze. Now he was chasing Ray Heindorf's secretary. Neither of the ladies seemed to mind.

He entertained the set with his impersonations of Billy Eckstine and Liberace and while recording the title song he switched in the middle of the take and finished it as Nat King Cole.

For the duet, "Dio Ti Giocondi" from the third act of *Otello*, the studio music department asked Lanza to help them select a singer from a number of fine operatic voices in Los Angeles. He insisted on Licia Albanese of the Metropolitan Opera. The studio didn't want the added expense, but Lanza got his way and Albanese was put under contract. She was grateful to him;

135

although a brilliant singer, she had never been paid by Hollywood standards.

RCA Victor used the sound track from the film for the album rather than rerecording the numbers, as they had done in the past. It was an unusually good sound track musically and technically.

But nothing could go serenely for long in Lanza's life. The pattern was now familiar. Mario would embark on a project enthusiastically. Before long the pressures would build and he would come apart. His "down" periods had become increasingly irrational and unstable to the point where his mental well-being was in jeopardy. With shooting on *Serenade* soon to start, Lanza fell into another of his depressions, this one more frightening than any of the others. His feelings of persecution, his mistrust of people who were trying to help him became extreme. When a blowup finally came it was, not surprisingly, triggered by Lanza's weight problem. As usual he had ballooned up during the prerecording sessions to give his voice power. The need to trim down rapidly to Hollywood star proportions—and the sniping in the press about his girth—got to him.

One day Betty, Terry, and columnist Lloyd Shearer were listening to his complaints about a newspaper item. "That's all they ever talk about. Lanza's fat!" He slammed the paper down and paced back and forth across the room.

Terry said, "Mario, forget it. Your public loves you. They just want to hear your voice."

Lanza jumped on the statement. "Sure. The voice. That's what *they* want.The voice. But what about me?"

Lloyd and Terry looked at one another, but said nothing. Betty tried to calm him. "Honey, don't be upset. We're only trying to tell you that you don't have to diet and make yourself nervous."

Lanza only grew angrier. "That's me on the screen and I'm the one they pick on. I'm the one they call names. I can't even get a sore throat without being crucified. Well, I'll soon be dead and then the truth will come out."

"Mario," Betty said.

"You're all against me," he cried. "I'm going for a drive."

"I'll go with you," Terry said.

"Stay here! What the hell are you, my shadow?" The three sat in stunned silence as Lanza went out and drove away.

None of them had ever seen him quite so distraught. Terry couldn't help thinking about that wild ride Lanza had taken him on. Shearer suggested that a psychiatrist friend of his at Payne-Whitney Clinic in New York might be able to help Lanza. They all agreed it would be a good idea. The trick would be to get Lanza, who wouldn't admit that anything was wrong with him, to go along with it.

He was still in a bad mood when he returned awhile later and found the three sitting where he had left them. "I just sang my heart out at the studio. None of you people understand. It's the voice. It does something. It comes from the toes. It pours out. I get into another world. Then I come back here and all I hear is how great the voice was and how fat the guy is and how egotistical and temperamental."

He rambled on, becoming incoherent. He seemed to be coming apart.

Shearer said, "Mario, we all want to help."

"Help! No one can help me!"

Tactfully Betty said, "Honey, you have to start shooting this picture soon. Why don't you, Terry, and Lloyd fly to New York. Lloyd has a friend who's a psychiatrist. You don't have to see him professionally. Just talk to him and let him assure you everything is fine, that you have nothing to fear from anybody. Would you do that for me?"

For a while he sat dejectedly. Then he roused himself and said, "Betty, if you want me to go, then I'll go. Maybe the change of scenery will relax me."

Lanza boarded the plane in disguise as "Fred Mason." The three men had a sleeper compartment for the overnight flight. Lanza took a sleeping pill and Terry and Shearer sat up discussing their plan. Lanza hadn't been told he was being taken to the Payne-Whitney Clinic; if he had known, he would have refused to go. To avoid publicity they decided to stay at Kathryn Reitzle's home until the visit to the clinic. Kathryn had followed Mario to work for him in Hollywood, at his insistence, but once she saw the inner workings of the film capital, she returned to New York to a world which, in her opinion, dealt in reality—not fantasy.

When they got to Reitzle's home, Lanza was glad to see his former secretary. But the nature of his conversation left no doubt in anyone's mind that they were doing the right thing. Lanza was still obsessed with the idea that everyone was out to get him.

"My life is in danger," he told Reitzle. "I can't take it any longer."

They waited for dark and then got a cab to the clinic. Terry waited in the outer office while Shearer accompanied Lanza in to see the psychiatrist. It didn't take long for the patient to realize that he was there for more than a friendly chat.

Shearer fled from the office. "You take care of him," he said to Terry. "He's angry as hell. I'm going back to the coast. I'll explain to Betty."

He escaped just as Lanza came barging out, shouting, "You bastards! This is a nuthouse!"

Outside Terry tried to get in the cab but Lanza, kicking and raving, wouldn't let him. "You railroaded me! They have bars on the windows!"

Meanwhile the cabbie was taking it all in. Lanza's hat and glasses had fallen off and it was easy to recognize him.

"Terry, leave me alone," Lanza said. "You're just like all the rest, out to get me."

"I can't leave you. Besides I have all the money and I'm hungry."

Lanza finally relented and Terry ordered the driver to pull away from the curb, as a crowd had begun to gather.

"Okay, Mister. As long as there's no trouble."

"No trouble, I promise. My friend's not feeling well."

"Your friend is Mario Lanza, isn't he?"

As a bizarre conclusion to the abortive trip to New York, Terry, Lanza, and the cabbie ended up at Nathan's Restaurant in Coney Island. It was winter and they stood outside in the cold, eating hot dogs and drinking root beer while the wind blew salt spray in from the ocean. Oddly, the cabbie had more luck than Shearer's psychiatrist friend at bringing Lanza out of his desperate mood. They discussed their families and laughed together.

The next morning the desperation was over. Lanza phoned Betty and told her to tell Shearer he wasn't angry. "He meant well. But I'm not sick. People are out to get me, that's all."

The conversation didn't quite reassure anyone that all was well.

Lanza's borderline paranoia was evident as shooting began on *Serenade*. The film would be made partly on location in San Miguel de Allende, Mexico, a small town 200 miles north of Mexico City, and at the Warner Brothers Studio in Burbank.

From the start he surrounded himself with his own people as a protective wall against "all those fuckers who are out to get me." His makeup man, Lou La Cava, was Italian and that gave him someone he could talk to in his parents' native tongue. He liked that. When Lanza spoke Italian he assumed that only he and the person he was speaking to knew what he was saying.

In Mexico he had the same old problem with his fans. People mobbed the railroad car he was riding in and security broke down. Reinforcements had to be sent for because even the police who were there to protect him became part of the mob seeking autographs or just wanting to touch Lanza.

He and his co-star, Spanish actress Sarita Montiel, attended the bullfight together. There was a bullfight scene in the film and technical director Pepe Ortiz wanted Lanza to see what a real *corrida de toros* was like. When the first bull was killed, the ear was cut off and presented to Lanza. He acknowledged the honor and bowed to the matador and the crowd. After the next kill, the matador tossed his hat and cape up to him. Lanza turned and presented the hat and cape to Sarita. The Mexicans loved it.

They would have been less appreciative of his perform-ance that night. Unable to reach his family because of bad telephone connections, he instead found a bottle of tequila and a young Mexican girl. When Lanza drank he sometimes became a little rough—too rough in this case. The following day Terry paid off the girl and her parents to keep down what could have become a major scandal, since the girl was underage.

Throughout the filming he seemed to be spoiling for a fight. One night he threw a party for the crew and some of the local V.I.P.'s. A wealthy Mexican landowner who spoke ex-cellent English started to tell an off-color joke about a bearded Jew. "Get that bigoted son-of-a-bitch out of here!" Lanza shouted; he had to be held back to keep from punching the guest.

Back in the studio at Burbank, California, his relationship with his co-star, Joan Fontaine, was cool at best. She found Lanza's often crude behavior and language hard to take. Fontaine was not the kind of woman to be amused when someone pinched her bottom.

Consequently she was quickly relegated to that rapidly increasing group of people who were out to get Lanza.

"There's always somebody around waiting for Lanza to make a mistake," he told Terry. "I'll bet Fontaine would love to see me louse up my lines. I'll fix her."

Lanza's retaliation consisted of eating garlic cloves before the two did a love scene. Fontaine never let on that she even noticed. Not so with former co-star Kathryn Grayson who slapped his face when he tried a similar tactic during one of their romantic scenes.

Lanza's pugnacious attitude almost got him into a fight with a real fighter. Former heavyweight champion Max Baer was in town and Lanza invited him to dinner. George Eiferman, Terry, Betty, and Lanza's parents were all there, enjoying

140

Baer's ring stories. During the conversation Lanza remarked that Rocky Marciano was the greatest fighter of them all.

Baer disagreed. "He had no one to fight. He was a cheese champ."

"He knocked out Joe Louis and Louis kayoed you, Max."

Baer, stung by the remark, repeated his statement. "Rocky was a cheese champ. If I fought him, I'd hold him off with my left and counter underneath with a right." He stood up to demonstrate his strategy.

Lanza bounded to his feet. "Max, I'll tell you what. I'll be Rocky and you show me what you mean."

Baer made a feint and started to explain when Lanza bobbed and weaved and let a left hook fly, hitting him on the shoulder. Baer spun, tripped and fell on the couch, almost on top of Betty. George and Tony grabbed him and Terry went for Lanza. "Cut it out, Mario," he said.

Baer shrugged it off good-naturedly. "Hey, I'm the fighter. You're supposed to sing, not swing."

The *Serenade* set wasn't a total battleground. Lanza got along well with fellow actors Vince Edwards and Vincent Price, as well as with Licia Albanese and Sarita Montiel. Nevertheless Terry felt they were lucky to complete the film without a disaster.

Jack Warner was pleased and wired Lanza: "I know it will be the best picture you have ever appeared in."

Warner had reason to be happy. His studio had successfully met what by now was known as a major challenge to a Hollywood studio. It had filmed a Mario Lanza picture.

Mario had his fun, however, during the filming of *Serenade*. Henry Blanke, the producer, was simultaneously producing another picture, *Sincerely Yours*, which starred Liberace. Every day on the set Blanke would regale Mario with the wonders of Liberace—what a marvelous boy he was and how their friendship had grown. Mario decided to put some zest into that relationship.

Several times in the evening, after returning from a long

day's filming, he would call Blanke on the telephone and in perfect Liberace diction and accent would proceed to call Blanke every name in the book, telling him what a no good so-and-so he was. The following day when Blanke would be with Mario on the set he would discuss the calls with Mario. "You know that kid Liberace, I don't know what's bothering that boy. At night he must drink. He wakes me up in the middle of my sleep and says such terrible things on the telephone. I see him in the daytime and he is so sweet. Such a nice boy to let alcohol get to him that way." Mario loved the charade.

Shortly after the film was completed, having little or nothing to do, he drank. When he drank he remembered that Sheilah Graham had written something unflattering about him. To get even, he called her. Knowing that the late George Sanders was a close friend, he took on the character of Sanders and berated her for a full fifteen minutes, giving vent to every filthy female name he could think of. She never suspected it wasn't George and couldn't understand why he would attack her.

Mario, however, did not limit such attacks to the telephone. One night while listening to a playback of the *Otello* duet with some friends, among whom was actor/singer Howard Keel, Howard, not aware that Mario was sitting directly behind him, commented: "Only a mad man can sing like that."

Taking offense, Mario barked, "Howard, let me give you a bit of advice. Get mad, fuck up, and you'll be a better singer." It was embarrassing—but that was Mario.

17

One evening Lanza, Terry and a friend went to Al Teitlebaum's store. After getting no response to their knocks on the back door, they turned to leave and noticed Teitlebaum's car parked in its usual space. Lanza knocked again, louder. Still no response. The men went around front and knocked.

Al Teitlebaum opened the front door calmly and let the men in. He said, "Our store was just robbed. We were all tied up."

Within minutes the place was overrun with police. Lanza got out in a hurry before anybody recognized him. The next day the morning dailies headlined: BIG BEVERLY HILLS FUR ROBBERY. From the beginning the authorities suspected something fishy. It just didn't look like a robbery. An investigation brought out the fact that Teitlebaum was heavily in debt. Lanza was called as a witness before the Grand Jury and the newspapers once again made him the center of the story. The Los Angeles *Examiner* said: "In a surprise move, District Attorney S. Ernest Roll today called Mario Lanza before the grand jury to tell what he knew about the $280,000 reported fake fur robbery at the salon of the opera singer's friend, Al Teitlebaum."

Teitlebaum and two associates were indicted. He was later found guilty and served a year in prison. Lanza stuck by him. "I have confidence in Al Teitlebaum and believe him to be innocent."

Because of appeals and delays, it was several years before Teitlebaum went to jail and he continued to serve as Lanza's manager.

Shortly after the Teitlebaum scandal, during a late spring rain storm, another unsettling incident arose. Colleen and Ellisa wanted to go outside. Dressed in boots and raincoats, they were permitted to play in front of the house on the circle driveway. Their nurses were nearby. Betty was out of the house shopping and Mario was in the living room with Terry. Suddenly they heard screams and rushed outside where they discovered the family St. Bernard towering over Ellisa who was flat on the ground, her little face frozen by fright. Colleen, on top of the family car, was screaming at the top of her lungs.

Both men leaped into action; Terry charged the dog and hit him hard in the jaw with his fist. While the stunned animal staggered about, he picked up Ellisa and, cuddling her in his arms, rushed for the house. The dog followed, grabbing his shirttail in its jaws and ripping the shirt from his back as he managed to get Ellisa safely into the house and slam the door behind them.

The St. Bernard then attacked Colleen. Mario held him off and yelled out, "Give him a steak! Give him a steak!" A maid opened the door and flung a top sirloin some distance away. Mario escaped with Colleen into the house as the dog attacked the raw meat. It was later learned that during several days of rain nobody had thought to feed the dog. Fortunately, no one was injured—but Lanza and Terry's quick reaction had saved the children from serious injury and possibly worse.

Serenade was released and expected to do well at the box office. In addition to favorable reviews, the picture also inspired a telegram to Lanza from Rocky Marciano.

> Serenade *perfectly wonderful. Loved every note.*
> *You're a real champ. When you hit 'em, they stay hit.*

Not long afterward Lanza got a phone call from Marciano, who said he was in town with a couple of friends and wanted to drop by for a visit.

When they got there, the heavyweight champion introduced his two friends as Mr. Lucchese and Mr. Lombardo. Terry recognized Lucchese by name immediately. He was known in underworld circles as "Three Fingers Brown," a close friend of deported Mafia kingpin Lucky Luciano. Terry was a little surprised that Marciano would be in the company of known mobsters.

The men sat down with Lanza in the big parlor. They talked and drank awhile and finally Marciano said, "Mario, I know you've been having financial difficulties and I know what it's like. I've been there myself."

Lanza nodded—so did Lucchese and Lombardo—and, after taking another drink, he began to go into his problems. Lucchese became impatient and got directly to the point.

"Mario, you work for me, your troubles are over. Right, Rocky?" Marciano agreed and Lucchese continued. "We split down the middle. Our own record and production company and all the fringe benefits. In other words, you play ball with us, we take care of you. All you have to do is perform."

Lanza listened quietly but Terry saw what was coming. Lanza hated the Mob. It was unthinkable that he would go for such a proposition. What worried Terry was Lanza's inability to hold his temper, an almost insane temper, especially when it was fueled by a few drinks, and Lucchese and Lombardo were not the studio executive types that were the usual targets of his outbursts.

Terry cleared his throat and tried to change the conversation but Lanza gave him a stern look. He waited until Lucchese finished. Then he said, "Is that your proposition?"

"That's it," Lucchese said. "No strings. All out front. Nice and clean."

With deadly calm Lanza turned to Marciano. "You really

145

surprise me, Rocky. To think I actually looked up to you."

Marciano, realizing he had made a miscalculation, wouldn't look him in the eye.

Lanza then turned to Lucchese, who was clearly unprepared for what was happening. He pointed a finger at him and in a slow, deliberate voice said, "No cheap lousy hood can buy me."

Lucchese blanched and Lombardo, who had been feeding himself assiduously, froze with a cracker and cheese dip in his pudgy fingers. Before either could react, Lanza was on his feet.

"Get out!" he yelled. "I'm no fucking puppet! This is God's voice! It passes through here!" He grabbed his throat for emphasis. "I wasn't made with a finger, you assholes! I was made with a prick! You think I don't know your kind? When I was a kid, my uncle was shot down in the streets of South Philadelphia for getting mixed up with your kind. I watched him die. My grandfather chased bums like you out of his store when they came around offering 'protection.'"

At that instant Betty, groggy from her usual mixture of booze and drugs, staggered out of her bedroom and yelled down the stairs, "Keep it quiet down there! Get the hell out of my house, all of you! You're going to wake up the babies and then I'll come down and throw you out personally!"

For the next few minutes bedlam reigned as Lanza berated the mobsters and told his wife to shut up, while Betty blasted them all. Marciano, thoroughly embarrassed, got his two friends out as quickly as possible, but at the door Lucchese had a parting word.

"Listen, you fat slob. You don't know who you're talking to. Keep your big mouth shut or I'll shut it permanently."

"You don't scare me!" Lanza went for Lucchese and Terry had to hold him back.

"You'll be hearing from us!" Lombardo shouted over his shoulder as he retreated.

Lanza told him what he could do with himself and closed the door with a violent kick.

146

Lanza's reaction to the Mob's proposition would have been negative under any condition, but alcohol had without a doubt given it its distinctively violent character. In the ten years Terry had worked for him he had seen Lanza's drinking get progressively out of hand. Lanza drank when he was happy in order to sustain his mood. He drank when he was depressed to dull the pain. He realized deep down that it was doing him no good, but his compulsive nature made it difficult for him to give it up.

For some time he had been taking Antabuse to prevent him from drinking. His doctor informed him that to drink while ingesting the drug would make him extremely ill. Betty would stand by and watch him take the pills to make sure he didn't spit them out. He would drink anyway and become sick, vomiting and developing blinding headaches. The result was more depression, but he would not give up the alcohol.

He refused to attend AA meetings although he had friends in the industry who went regularly. "I'm not a drunk," he argued. "AA is for alcoholics. I just drink a little bit too much sometimes."

The most he had ever done was to check into Las Encinas Sanitarium in Pasadena once for a brief stay before doing the first Chrysler television special. He was there ostensibly to lose weight for the upcoming show but that was only part of the reason; the other part was that he wanted to get off the bottle for a while. Las Encinas had helped a lot of Hollywood stars dry out. The institution had private rooms, doctors and nurses around the clock, and tight security. During his stay he was surprised to see a familiar white-haired gentleman strolling outside one day with his hands clasped behind his back and his head bent low. It was Spencer Tracy, and Lanza felt a little better knowing he was not the only star with a drinking problem.

Lanza's drinking went hand-in-hand with his womanizing. For two summers he had a beach house at Trancas Beach near Malibu. The beach house gave him a chance to get away from Betty and be with the guys. Betty was allowed to come down on weekends with the children, but during the week the beach house was a bachelor pad for Mario and his friends.

One day a photographer friend asked Lanza if it was okay to shoot some cheesecake shots with an actress who was in love with Mario. Lanza said, "Fine. If she loves me, maybe I'll learn to love her, too." The young actress, Inger Stevens, later a T.V. and film star (and eventually a suicide) came out to the beach house—the only female in the house. After the cheesecake session on the beach the photographer brought her in and Lanza showed a pornographic film. Everybody was drinking and getting high. The actress, who was sitting on the piano bench wearing a skimpy bikini, asked Lanza to sing.

"I'll do something better for you," he said. He got up and walked over to her, lifted her up on the piano and slipped off her bikini bottom. He spread her legs apart and said, "For the first time Lanza's high note will come out of a woman's body." He put his mouth over her bottom and sang into her vagina. In his drunken state he couldn't understand why she wasn't particularly delighted with his performance.

Sober, Lanza was usually the opposite, a soft-spoken and gentle man who thought mostly of his family. Although he was a busy man, he always had time for his children. He would sit with them for hours playing games or watching kiddie shows on television. He loved to sneak off to the pier with them to watch the old men fish and the sea gulls dive for anchovies. He was often asked to ride in the annual Hollywood Christmas Parade with his children but he always declined. Instead he took Colleen and Lisa to the corner of Las Palmas Street and Hollywood Boulevard to watch the celebrity floats go by, like any ordinary papa in the crowd.

Both his agents and business managers thought it would be a sound move if Lanza took his family to live in Europe for a few years to save money and avoid heavy taxes. Lester Welch, a producer who was the son-in-law of the famous European movie-maker Gregor Rabinovich, put together an idea for a film which MGM agreed to finance and distribute. The picture was *The Seven Hills of Rome*. Roy Rowland was to be the director, Georgie Stoll the musical director, and his old friend Gene Ruggiero would be the editor. Actual shooting was to begin in Rome early in May 1957. Lanza would leave in April to start prerecording for the picture.

Elated that MGM had "finally seen the light," Lanza was enthusiastic about making the film and being able to take his family to Rome. Preparations to leave the United States began. There was the matter of passports for everybody, shots, selling the house, storing furniture, and hiring a new girl to help with the children on the way to Europe. Once they were in Italy, help would be easier to find and much cheaper and the girl could be sent back home. Georgie Stoll and Irving Aaronson came over each day, going over ideas for the music and the film.

The Lanzas settled at the Villa Badoglio, which had once been owned by Benito Mussolini, who had presented it as a gift to Field Marshal Badoglio for his leadership against the Ethiopians in the one-sided war waged against them by Italy. The villa was situated in the most exclusive residential section of Rome and, although within the city boundaries, it was always very quiet. The grounds extended the length of a tree-lined street. The entrance was guarded by ornate iron gates with a security guard who occupied a small office to one side. The home was palatial, consisting of forty rooms, including a fully equipped gymnasium. The ceilings and floors, of mosaic marble, shone like polished mirrors. It was exquisitely furnished with French and Italian antiques. There was a separate wing for the children and their entourage, which included governesses, nurses, and tutors. The estate had swimming pools and tennis courts and large garages for the Lanza fleet of cars.

Lanza behaved like a man who had found freedom after years of bondage. He boasted, "I left all my problems behind in Hollywood. When I walked down the gangplank in Naples and set foot in Europe for the first time, I knew that a new life faced me."

He was bitter about Hollywood and his years there. "In

Hollywood they expect everything about you to be printed in their trashy magazines like *Confidential*. I have always believed that a star does not wash his dirty linen in public. The one obligation a star has to his public is performance—that is all."

As for his fights with the studios and temperamental behavior, he shrugged: "I think the real answers to such charges lie in my current situation. Metro has a fortune tied up in *The Seven Hills of Rome*. If I were difficult, would they be taking a chance on me again?"

The Vatican's Auditorium Angelico was used for the prerecordings on *The Seven Hills of Rome*. Georgie Stoll conducted the Italian National Radio Symphony, and Irving Aaronson assisted. In spite of his dedication to classical music, the ham in Lanza always came out. For this picture he recorded impersonations of Perry Como, Frankie Laine, Dean Martin, and Louis Armstrong, a gimmick that became one of the highlights of both the film and the album. He also sang, in his own voice, "Seven Hills of Rome," "Italiano Calypso," "Lolita," "Questa o Quella," "Arrivederci Roma," and "Come Dance with Me."

Only one unpleasant incident marred the filming. A courier arrived from Rome with a message from the producer, Goffredo Lombardo, to close down the picture for four days. Lanza said no. "Let's get this film finished. I have things to do."

The courier said, "I'm sorry, but Lombardo says you, Lanza, have to go to Rome and sing for a special benefit."

"What the hell do you mean? This picture is the only benefit I'm singing for this year—to benefit Mario Lanza."

"He insists."

"I don't give a damn. Go tell him Lanza insists."

Lombardo had his way. The set was closed down. Lanza did sing, under protest, but instead of coming back to work, he went on a two-week binge and was fined $35,000 for holding up the production. Lombardo could close down the picture, but not Lanza. Lanza said, "It was worth $35,000."

He continued his partying. The lavish villa was open to

one and all every day. Betty hired ten servants and, using uppers and downers to keep herself going, was able to play hostess on a daily basis.

A London *Daily Mirror* newspaperman described Lanza during an interview: "coal black hair, towering over a sallow sensitive face. . . ." The sallow face was the giveaway. Lanza's high living was catching up with him.

He barely made it through the picture, ignoring his doctors' advice about diet and abstinence from alcohol. "What is an Italian without pasta and vino?" he asked. "I am an Italian. If I must die, then so be it. I will die happy."

18

n Rome Lanza didn't hesitate to discuss his past differences with MGM. "They always wanted my songs recorded several weeks before production began. Then, while sets and costumes were being prepared, I had about four weeks to trim down to look like Mr. America for the cameras." He bitterly complained, "There is no sentiment in Hollywood when it comes to money."

But now Hollywood was part of the past. Europe was before him. He wanted to do a tour in England after *The Seven Hills of Rome* was completed. Learning that Callinicos was separated from his wife and son, and without ties in the United States, he and Betty put through a trans-Atlantic call and convinced him to come to Rome to accompany them on the tour, to start in mid-November.

Lanza took London by storm. He was mobbed on his arrival on the Golden Arrow from Italy. The surge of the crowd literally knocked him off his feet, and only quick action by assigned bodyguards saved him from injury. It didn't bother Lanza. After his acrimonious exit from America such a triumphant arrival buoyed him up.

Everything went smoothly until the British press got down to business at a press conference. When a reporter asked Lanza, "What do you weigh these days?" he blew his top.

"Can't you people ask an artist a sensible question?" he answered. "My weight is my business. All my career that's all you newspaper guys want to know about me. I was born big. I live big. I sing big. Everything I do is big. Print that!"

The following day he was referred to in the London papers as The Tubby Tenor, The Roly-Poly Tenor, and The Temperamental Tenor.

Sulking, Lanza called off his afternoon rehearsal. Callinicos went to the London Palladium and rehearsed the orchestra without him. A crowd had gathered to watch the rehearsal and soon rumors spread: Lanza was ill, he was drunk, he had cancelled the concert.

When Callinicos returned to the hotel he looked tired and nervous. "Here," Lanza said, "have a drink. Relax. We'll do the show."

Callinicos was noticeably relieved as Lanza poured two glasses of champagne. *"La vita e breve, la morte viene,"* he said, toasting his conductor. (Life is very short and death will come.)

Lanza was never in better voice than on the night of his Royal Command Performance for Queen Elizabeth. The 2,500-seat Palladium was jammed. Judy Garland shared the program with him but received little notice in the press. Lanza was last on the program and the applause seemed to go on forever.

"Mr. Lanza," the Queen said when they were introduced later, "I never knew such big sounds could come from the human throat."

Mario quickly responded, "I never thought so young and gracious a lady could rule so large a country." He flirted with every woman—even the Queen of England.

Lanza and his wife returned to Rome for Christmas while Columbia Concerts worked out a European tour. On New Year's Eve, as was the custom in Italy, he joined with the servants in throwing noisy objects out the window in celebration.

The New Year brought the first reports on the American release of *The Seven Hills of Rome*. Even his former critics praised his performance and said it was one of his best. Lanza was amused to see how popular he was becoming with the

American press now that he was out of the country.

His second tour of England was also a success, highlighted by three consecutive concerts at Royal Albert Hall, where each event was a sellout to 8,000 Lanza fans. RCA Victor recorded an album in the great hall, which is 273 feet in length, with a glass dome 155 feet high, the largest assembly hall in Great Britain.

One English critic said, "That Lanza's British audience knew it was getting its money's worth is clear from the fervent applause and cheers. Each song is performed differently. Puccini is not Scarlatti. English Music Hall is not Hollywood, and no one knew it better than Mario Lanza."

He had a severe attack of gout prior to the third Royal Albert Hall concert, but after a shot from a doctor he went on and sang his heart out. Nevertheless, diabetes, gout, and phlebitis continued to plague him during the tour. He refused to stick to a sensible diet and abstain from wine and liquor. He survived on injections, and a rubber stocking covered his inflamed leg. One such injection, probably from a bad needle, resulted in blood poisoning. Supporting himself with a cane, he finished the tour, but finally bowing to common sense, he cancelled the West German tour that was to follow England.

On his return to Rome he entered the hospital for treatment. One British newspaper reported, "There was nothing wrong with Mario Lanza. He's been seen in nightclubs in Rome." It so infuriated him that he insisted the German tour be rebooked.

The exuberant German audiences mobbed him after each performance, jumping up on the stage and wrestling him to the ground. It was the same in Stuttgart, Baden-Baden, and other stops. He began to fear the crowds; they had always made him nervous anyway. In Hamburg he was scheduled to sing at Festive Hall. It was a sellout crowd, loud and boisterous. Lanza's fear surfaced and he magnified a sniffle into a cold that supposedly had him so weak and hoarse he could neither stand nor speak. He gave out interviews afterward to the effect that he sounded like Andy Devine, but no one took him seriously. Cancellation of this appearance, following his widely reported cancellation of the earlier German tour, resulted in chaos. The police were called in to quell the near riot that took place in Hamburg over his failure to appear. One reporter referred to him as "an American swine." Insulted by the remark, he cancelled his next two concerts in Germany.

He left Germany and returned to England, where he toured by train, but his heart was no longer in it. There was nothing wrong with the voice; he had lost his desire to sing outside the recording studio. Despite his lack of interest, though, the tour was a success. The Lanza name was as big a draw as ever.

With Lanza and Betty constantly busy, sometimes a whole week would pass without their children seeing them. Occasionally, though, they would make a point of setting aside an afternoon to be alone with the children. Two overstuffed chairs would be set in the large hallway and Lanza and his wife would sit there like royalty in a throne room. The servants learned to keep a safe distance, having been advised of the privacy of these sessions, and were compelled to find indirect routes from one part of the villa to another that would avoid the hall. It was the nearest thing to a normal family life that the children had in Rome.

The hallway, which was ten or fifteen feet wide and very long, served another purpose. The children, who were raised like little potentates, used it for a bicycle path. They would ride their bikes up and down the polished marble floors and the servants sometimes had to get out of the way pretty fast.

Lanza and Betty had well-grounded fears that the children might become victims of kidnap attempts. Yet, the villa was always full of people, many of them strangers. With so many visitors coming and going, nobody would have been able to tell a kidnapper from a nonkidnapper. One stranger who was almost run down by the speeding bikes was Mr. Luciano, whom the children remembered for his odd first name: Lucky.

From time to time throughout his life in Rome Lanza was approached by shady characters who wanted him to do concerts or become involved in "business" deals. Luciano, the notorious Mafia boss who had been deported from the United States, was one of these. Lanza told them all he wasn't interested. But Luciano was persistent; he kept showing up at the villa. Lanza liked all sorts of people and couldn't help being interested in the famous gangster. But whenever the conversation got around to "business," he would lose his temper. The children sometimes heard their father and Mr. Luciano arguing late at night, and Lanza invariably ended such discussions by telling Luciano to get out.

The possibility of being kidnapped wasn't the only danger the children faced. One night Lanza made the mistake of taking them to *Aida* at the local opera house. At the entrance he was mobbed by autograph seekers. Once inside they hid until the lights went down and then found their seats. In the middle of the second act someone spotted Lanza and people began to descend on their box. At the height of the crush Damon's nurse had to throw herself over him to protect him. She was badly bruised and required medical attention.

After that the children continued going to the opera but never with their father.

A new film was scheduled, and Lanza abruptly cancelled a proposed South African tour. He used the film as an excuse, but the truth was that since the incident at *Aida* he was more frightened than ever of crowds. The film was titled *For the First Time* and his co-star was Zsa Zsa Gabor.

Bloated as he always was prior to beginning a film, Lanza was nevertheless at a prime weight for recording. He recorded the songs for the film at the Rome Opera House accompanied by 160 musicians from the Rome Opera Orchestra. It was the toughest audience he would ever face. They had never heard Lanza sing in person and most of them believed that his voice was manufactured by Hollywood sound technicians. Being an

American, he couldn't be very good; only Italians born in Italy could sing. Everybody knew that.

Lanza had his own preconceptions. If you can't sing, the Italians are the rudest audiences in the world. If you thrill them, they're the most demonstrative. Before beginning, he winked at musical director George Stoll and said, "This is like facing the firing squad. One mistake and it's all over."

Stoll assured him there was nothing to worry about, but Lanza was sweating profusely. To warm up he sang "O sole mio," a familiar Italian favorite with which he felt comfortable. After the recording was completed, no one moved. Total silence hung over the hall.

Lanza looked askance at Stoll, as if to say, "What did I do wrong?"

Then suddenly the place erupted with bravos. The musicians stood on their chairs. Music stands fell and music scattered. "Bravo!" Lanza, wringing wet, bowed deeply and thanked them in Italian. "Grazie, grazie!" He was a success with the countrymen of his ancestors.

Ricardo Vitale, General Director of the Rome Opera, was present for the recording session and begged him, "Won't you sing for us? Open our opera season."

"When I can have my parents here, then I'll do it," Lanza said.

They went back to work and he recorded the songs for the film: "Come Prima" (a new song), a Tarantella (written by Georgie Stoll), "O sole mio," a Neopolitan Dance, a Mazurka, "Pineapple Pickers" (a rock and roll tune), "The Hofbrauhaus Song," "O Mon Amour" (in French) "Vesti la giubba," Finale from *Otello*, Act 1 from *Aida*, "Ichliebe Dich," and "Ave Maria." The songs were later released by RCA Victor in an album entitled *Mario Lanza: For the First Time*.

Lanza had the children on the set almost every day. They loved being with their father and watching him work. It was a rare treat for them.

Terry was in the United States with Mary and Tony but

talked with Lanza constantly on the phone. Mario seemed to be coming to terms with some of his demons. He took setbacks more philosophically and showed a renewed attachment to life.

For the First Time was completed without a hitch. A post-production party was held at Lanza's villa and everybody who was anybody in Rome attended, including his co-star. Zsa Zsa had gone to a beauty salon that day to have her hair bleached. By the time she arrived at the party, it had turned green. Her amused chagrin only added to the party's festive mood.

"After we finish dubbing the picture," Lanza told his wife, "I want to take a real vacation with you and the children."

Betty shook her head in amusement. "Mario, I've been waiting to hear you say that since our babies were born."

"I mean it. We'll take our second honeymoon, Betsy. Only this time, just you, me, and the children—no servants."

The vacation seemed a long way off. Work was already beginning on a new film to be called *Granada*. Another company wanted to do an original picture, *Laugh, Clown, Laugh*. Pontiac Motors wanted him to do a television production to be shot in Italy and shown in the United States. When he received the television proposal he immediately phoned Mary and Tony and said, "I'm back on top again. When I do this show I'll send you the biggest Pontiac they have."

In spite of the heavy work schedule, Lanza kept his word about the vacation. At Christmas the family went to St. Moritz. The children had never seen snow before and it was the first time they had been free of servants and nurses. It was a first for their parents, too—no agents, no interviews, no music to study, just relaxing and playing, learning to ice skate and having snowball fights, the happiest month and a half the family had spent together.

Late one night after the children had been put to bed, Lanza and Betty sat in front of the fireplace and held hands. "You know," he said, "I'd almost forgotten what it was like to be myself and have fun. It's been a long time."

Betty was also enjoying one of her rare moments of complete happiness.

They returned to Rome filled with plans for next year's vacation. There was a letter waiting from Dora Friedman, a young girl with polio who lived in South Africa. Dora was sad that Lanza had cancelled his tour. He sat down and wrote her a personal letter, explaining how sorry he was that he was unable to come and promising her he would make a special record for her, one that would not be sold in any stores anywhere in the world. He promised to make a dedication on the recording so that if anyone doubted it was made especially for her she could hear it from his own voice. He ended the letter by saying, "I appreciate your loyalty very much."

Lanza was certain he would do everything he promised: the recording for Dora, the vacations with Betty and the kids.

Having just finished a film, he was a fairly trim 200 pounds, about ten pounds over his filming weight, and in spite of his ailments he was bursting with energy. At 38 he felt his voice was just starting to mature.

He wrote Mary and Tony about life in Rome. "I'm having a ball over here. When I get home in the evening, I can go out to a party and still feel like working at eight in the morning. It differs from Hollywood in that it is not all business/business. The Italians know how to relax. It is not all "Gimmie, gimmie, gimmie."

In closing, he shared his bright outlook for the future. "I feel like going on forever and forever. I never want to quit. Now I know what I want. I want to live! I want to take my voice all over the world—the Middle East, Far East—even Russia. I want to put opera on film for theatres and schools or hospitals—for anyone who wants to see it. I'd like to create a foundation for that purpose. I know what they will say: 'He's crazy.' So what's new? If you don't believe in opera, you don't believe in anything."

Lanza had always loved recording, and in Italy he became obsessed with it. RCA Victor asked him to do an album of Caruso favorites and then decided to make it a double album.

One side would be Lanza, the other side Caruso. They felt giving people a chance to compare both voices in one package had surefire sales potential.

RCA assigned Paul Baron to conduct, and for the first time in his professional career Lanza didn't insist on his own conductor. Callinicos, miffed and disappointed, deserted him and Rome, and went to Greece. Baron and Lanza started rehearsals for the album but in mid-rehearsal Lanza had another idea. Remembering the Neapolitan songs that his mother had sung to him as a boy, he persuaded RCA to let him do that album first. Then, he promised, he would do the Caruso album.

Lanza got his way, and Italy's popular conductor Franco Ferrara (Franco Potenza directed the chorus) was selected to conduct the album, which was simply entitled: *Mario*.

The album was successful both artistically and financially. Lanza sang the songs in such perfect Neapolitan dialect that even the Italian musicians had difficulty believing he had never studied in Italy.

In his new mood Lanza missed his mother and father more than ever. "I can't stand it any longer," he told Mary one night on the phone. "I want you to both come over here and bring Grandpop with you. I'm very lonesome for all of you."

Tony was sick and begged off, but he told Mary to go ahead. She did, along with Grandpop and Betty's mother, May. Lanza hadn't seen his mother in two years. After the tearful greeting at the airport they drove slowly through Rome to his villa. He pointed out all the places of interest along the way. Mary noticed some men urinating against a wall. She said, "Look at those men, Fred. What slobs. In America they would be put in jail for indecent exposure."

Lanza laughed. "You'll see a lot of that in Italy. It's a custom."

Mary had another surprise when she got to the palace her son called home. She spoke to Damon and Marc in English and received very little response. They looked puzzled. Lanza

160

explained. "Better speak Italian, Mom, or they won't understand you at all."

Callinicos, who had been so upset over Paul Baron's conducting for Mario, returned to Rome at Lanza's request. They recorded an original stereo album of Rudolph Friml's *The Vagabond King*. The entire family sat in the control booth as Lanza recorded the album in six hours straight, from five in the afternoon until eleven that night. It was a hard day's work but everybody was happy with the results.

Grandpop Salvatore had not been to Italy in over 20 years and Lanza knew he would never get back there again, so he did everything possible to make his stay a real homecoming. He saw that his grandfather had his shot of scotch every morning, and at dinner nobody lifted a fork ahead of him. It pleased Lanza to see his family coming together in a traditional manner. When Mary got ready to return to America, Lanza hid his grandfather's passport, wanting to keep him in Italy. When the old man questioned him about it, Lanza said, "That's too bad. Now you can't go back to America. You have to stay here."

The entire family went to the airport to see Mary off. Betty's mother stayed, as did Salvatore. Lanza, kissing his mother good-bye, said, "Mom, come back for Christmas and bring Pop and Terry with you. You and I must do an album together, so think of some Neapolitan songs that we both know from my boyhood."

Before she boarded the plane, she cautioned him about some of his associates. "Freddie, stay away from people like Luciano. He means you no good and can only cause you problems. You've always said you would never work with those people. Please don't start now."

"Don't worry, Mom. I'm not for sale. You know that."

"Yes, but I heard your arguments with that man. I thought you would fight. You don't need him around your house, or your children."

He assured her she had nothing to worry about.

19

Without the knowledge of those closest to him, Lanza made arrangements, through Lucky Luciano, to do a charity performance in Naples. Luciano's persistence had broken his resistance. All his life he had been approached by underworld figures who tried to cash in on his talent and popularity and each time he had rebuffed them. In Italy he finally succumbed, but he made it plain, "Only one concert, and only for charity."

A few days before the concert, Lanza didn't show up for a scheduled rehearsal. The promoters were furious, especially when they found him in a small cafe drinking wine and singing at the top of his lungs for the benefit of four or five afternoon alcoholics. Later that evening two men came to the villa and warned him: Show up for the concert or something bad would happen. Betty, overhearing them, stormed into the study and ordered them out of the house. "How dare you talk to Mario Lanza like a servant. Get out!"

"It's okay, Betsy. Don't worry," Lanza said.

The men left, but at the door one of them turned and again cautioned him. "If you don't show, you'll never appear in public again."

Betty insisted on knowing what was going on. Lanza was never very successful lying to his wife. He leveled with her, explaining about the concert's purpose and telling her who had lured him into it.

"My God, Mario," Betty said, "how could you do a thing like that? You promised me, you promised your mother—on your children's heads you promised."

He shrugged and looked the other way.

It was clear to Betty that he felt he had done the wrong thing but didn't see how he could get out of it. A day later he found an excuse, perhaps subconsciously. He had recently completed a new recording of "The Lord's Prayer" and was listening to a playback in his study, worrying about the concert, when Betty came in.

Looking up, sweat pouring down his face, he said, "Betsy, I don't feel good."

She thought he might be having a heart attack. "Are you having chest pains?"

He shook his head. "No. Nothing like that, but my leg is bothering me. I think it's the weight. I've got to start pre-recordings for *Granada* and I want to lose about fifteen pounds. I won't be able to do that benefit show in Naples. I'd better check with Dr. Morica and go into the clinic for a thorough going over—get off my leg for a few days."

"Are you trying to sign your own death warrant?" she said. "Mario, those people don't fool around. You never should have agreed to do the concert if you didn't intend to go through with it. This isn't MGM you're walking out on."

He dismissed the problem. "Things like that only happen in the movies, Betsy. My name is too big for anybody to try to do something to me. My God, there'd be an investigation around the world. No, those people don't want that kind of publicity." He shifted in his chair to take the weight off his bad leg. "Tell you what," he said. "You go for me. I'll start now to autograph boxes of albums which you can give out free."

It was useless to argue with him. He had made up his mind not to do the concert, and going into the hospital gave him an alibi. "Look, you have your mother and Grandpop with you. Don't worry. Everything is going to be all right. I'll see you every day and we'll talk on the phone. In no time I'll be back home and doing the prerecordings for *Granada*. Get some rest, go to the concert, and then stay home with the children. Nobody will bother you."

The following day, without fanfare, Lanza entered the Valle Guila Clinic. He was put on an intravenous program, a new method of weight-reducing therapy that involved injections of urine from pregnant women. His chauffeur accompanied him and slept in the room to be close to him. A nurse was assigned to Lanza to protect him from hospital attendants running in and out seeking autographs. That was the extent of the security provided him.

From the hospital he called his parents. Mary couldn't understand why he was there. "You looked so good when I saw you. Are you sure you're sick?"

"Only my leg, Mom. They want to take some tests. I'll be home in a couple of days. Are you and Pop coming over for Christmas?"

"Yes. Your father can hardly wait. I keep telling him it's only two months, but you know how he is, he wants to leave right now." She laughed.

"Let me talk to Terry."

"Hi, Tiger," Terry said, "what's the good word?"

"The good word is, when are you going to give up that gym and come over here where you belong? If you were here, I'd be in shape and all of this wouldn't be necessary. You know me and my body better than anybody. You come on over for Christmas with Mom and Pop. We'll have a big reunion. I can show you around—and boy, do I know some girls for you."

"Same old Mario," Terry said, "I'll bet you've got a nurse in bed with you right now."

"Wish I did. The one I've got has starch in her veins."

Lanza thanked Terry for the sports books he had sent, including an issue of *Strength & Health* with Terry's picture on the cover. "You look pretty good. Must get a lot of rest."

"Sure I do," Terry laughed. "But don't worry, I'm arranging

for someone to take over for me at the gym and I'll be there with Mary and Tony for Christmas. That's a promise."

Everything seemed fine. But the next day the doctor phoned Betty with the surprising news that her husband had a bad heart.

"I dont believe it," she said. "Mario never had any heart problem in his life."

Immediately after, the chauffeur phoned her and whispered into the phone. The nurse had told him Lanza had pneumonia. Nothing had been said of a heart problem. Betty was mystified. But later that day the hospital told her that a cardiologist had confirmed the diagnosis.

"Hell," Lanza protested, "I'm as strong as a bull. I have no bad heart. In New York the doctors told me my heart was big and strong enough for two men. I have a leg problem. Just don't complicate things."

He got on the phone to Betty and began to complain. "I'm tired of this place already. I don't know what they're doing to me. I come in for a checkup on my leg and now I'm all rigged up with needles and crap. You know how much I hate needles."

Betty, thinking he should for once follow the doctor's orders, said, "Mario, the concert is in another day and I don't know what I'm going to do. Just do as the doctor says."

But he was back on the phone later in the day, sounding even more desperate. "Betsy, they keep telling me my heart is bad and they want to keep me here. I want to come home. I miss you and I miss the children."

"Mario, stop calling me every five minutes. There's nothing that I can do. Listen to the doctors and get some rest."

He began to cry. "Betsy, maybe this is the end. Remember, I always told you I wouldn't be around very long."

Betty, convinced he was just feeling sorry for himself, said, "Yes, I know, honey. Fifty years from now you'll say the same thing. Get some rest. When you come home you can spend a

165

lot of time with the children. In the meantime, let me get some work done. I'll let you know how the concert turns out."

The concert was a disaster. Betty brought along the albums, but they pacified no one. Outside the hall scalpers were selling tickets at five and ten times their price. Inside, a minor riot broke out when the people learned Lanza wasn't going to appear. They booed Betty and she was fortunate to escape unharmed. Afraid to tell Mario, she got in touch with his doctor. "I'm sure it'll be in all the papers, and the minute he sees it, he'll be upset and want to come home." The doctor said he would do what he could to keep Lanza in the hospital as long as was necessary.

But Lanza had already made up his mind to leave. The day after the concert he told his chauffeur to bring him a change of clothes. "Go to the house. Don't let anyone know what you're up to. Bring me something to wear and let's get the hell out of here before they kill me with all these injections."

The chauffeur went to the house and was confronted by Colleen Lanza. "Where is my father?" she asked, knowing the chauffeur never left him.

"He's at the doctor's office. I'm going to get him now."

"Is he ill?"

"No, no. Just tired."

The chauffeur, however, related in detail to the child's nurse what was going on. "He insists on coming home. He thinks they're trying to kill him. I've never see him so upset."

When he arrived back at the hospital with Lanza's clothes, he found Mario comatose with the intravenous needle still attached to his arm. He yelled for the nurse, who appeared from just outside the room. The chauffeur pointed wildly at the IV jar with the tube running down to the needle. There was no fluid in the jar and only air could be entering Lanza's body.

It was October 7, 1959. Betty, feeling a little bad about the way she had talked to Mario in their last telephone

166

conversation, had decided to go to the hospital to cheer him up. She was about to leave the villa when the phone rang. It was Dr. Silvestri, the children's doctor who happened to be at the hospital. Before he could say anything more than, "Hello, Betty, this is Dr. Silvestri," she interrupted him.

"Doctor, I want to talk to Mario."

"I'm sorry, Betty," he said, "but you won't be able to. Mario just died. I'm really sorry."

Betty let out a scream and dropped the telephone. Silvestri rushed to the villa and gave her a sedative.

There was immediate confusion as to the cause of Lanza's death. Some said he had been given a fatal injection, others that he had died of an embolism, an 'air bubble which had traveled from the empty IV jar to his heart. There was an unconfirmed report that two doctors had worked on Lanza for two or three hours, giving him mouth to mouth resuscitation. The hospital was unable to come up with an official version beyond vaguely attributing the death to Lanza's new reducing therapy, a practice not yet approved by the FDA in America.

Under the circumstances Betty couldn't help harboring suspicions of a more sinister cause.

Embalming bodies was not the practice in Italy. Since Lanza was an American citizen, however, a chemical was injected in his skin to keep as much color as possible. He was taken from the hospital to an undertaking establishment, where he was placed in a wooden coffin. The box was too small, and nobody thought of finding a larger one. Instead, they broke his ankles and turned his feet sideways. His shoulder bones were also broken and his torso crammed into the narrow coffin.

Without embalming, his stomach soon became bloated and in this condition he was put on display in the living room at the villa. The children had been kept in their quarters without any explanation. Colleen, as irrepressible as her father, slipped out an open window. Dropping several feet to the ground, she made her way around the side of the house and climbed through a living room window. She knew something was wrong. That morning before she went to school she had spoken to her father on the phone and he had assured her he would be home that day.

In the living room, which was half-lit by flickering candles at each end of the catafalque where Lanza's body lay, she saw her father. Recoiling in fright, she ran through the house screaming, "Daddy is dead! Daddy is dead!" Running out into the street, she collapsed and was carried back into the villa by a member of the household staff. All of the children took the death of their father extremely hard.

In California news of Lanza's death came to Terry Robinson by telephone from a friend Larry Kagan who was listening to the morning news on the radio.

Terry couldn't believe it. "It must be a mistake," he said.

"Put on your radio," the friend said. "It's all they're talking about."

Mary and Tony, awakened by the early phone call, called out from their bedroom, "Who is it, Terry? Is it for us?"

"Please go back to bed," he said. "It's nothing."

Terry's hand shook as he poured a cup of coffee and went to the kitchen radio. Mary appeared in the doorway. "What's wrong, Terry? Is it your mother? Is there something wrong with your mother?"

He waved her away. "Nothing's wrong. Go on back to bed and get some more sleep." She stood there as he turned the radio on.

Tony joined them. "I can't sleep. What's going on?"

At that moment the radio blared out, "Be My Love." Mary perked up. "Is that what it's about? Are they having a special broadcast with Freddie from Rome?"

Terry was unable to answer. An announcer broke in on the recording and said, "That was the voice of the late Mario Lanza who passed away today from a heart attack in Rome, Italy."

Mary screamed and passed out. Tony lost control and ran

into the street yelling, "Freddie! Freddie!" Within minutes neighbors, having heard the news, gathered at the Cocozza home to be with Mary and Tony.

Dr. Silvestri phoned from Rome and asked Mary to fly over immediately to be with the children. On the flight the captain announced that she was on the plane, and throughout the trip passengers kept coming up to her to offer sympathy.

On Saturday, October 10, after three days of lying in his villa, the stench of putrefaction overwhelming all but the most hardy, Lanza was given a funeral service at the Church of San Bellermino in Rome's exclusive Parioli district. The horse-drawn casket attracted thousands of unruly spectators; people were nearly trampled in the confusion. At the church the Reverend Paul Maloney, who had baptized each of Lanza's children, said the Mass. Although the family requested it, the church forbade the playing of Lanza's recordings. Instead a choir sang. It was a circus, anyway. A mob of photographers was on hand, some crawling under the casket and nearly toppling it from its stand.

Betty went through the service in a daze and afterwards Mary took over. Philadelphia wanted Lanza's body to be brought there and put on view. Mary, although against it, didn't wish to disappoint her son's home town. So the rest of the family went on to Los Angeles, arriving in the middle of the night with two dogs, a canary, and assorted servants, while Salvatore accompanied the body to Philadelphia. Thousands lined the streets, and one woman, a close friend of the family, suffered a fatal heart attack as she stood before the casket. Leonetti's Funeral Parlor remained open all night to accommodate the crowds that streamed by for one last glimpse of the now grotesquely discolored and distended remains of Lanza.

When the body arrived in Los Angeles it was so deteriorated that the funeral parlor requested a member of the family to come down and identify it. The duty fell to Terry, who brought along clean clothes to replace the old ones. He was angry that Lanza had been put on view in Philadelphia in such condition and, knowing that the Hollywood crowd would also want a show, he insisted that the undertakers and makeup artists "make Mario look like Mario." He was outraged by the small coffin which was beginning to split and creak, and had it replaced with an expensive copper casket.

Betty, numb with shock, mistrustful of the conflicting versions of her husband's death, had voiced her gravest suspicion to Terry. "I think the Mafia had something to do with it. I think they murdered Mario."

Terry was unwilling to believe this; it was too melodramatic. Why would the Mafia murder Mario Lanza? Betty told him about the concert he had backed out of to go to the hospital and about the two men who had come to the villa to threaten him.

"But they couldn't," Terry said. "They wouldn't. . . ." He thought of the time Lanza had thrown Lucchese and Lombardo out of his home. There had been threats then, too, but nothing had come of them.

"They said if he didn't make the concert, he'd never appear in public again. I was there. I heard them. I told them to get out of the house." Betty was distraught. "Nobody knows how Mario died. Either that, or they're afraid to say. And what about the nurse?"

"What nurse?"

"The one who was giving him the intravenous injections. She disappeared. Even the police can't find her."

Terry tried to think of a logical explanation, but Betty had more to tell him. "Our chauffeur disappeared too. The one who went to the hospital and found Mario dead. He loved Mario. Why would he just leave like that? Nobody knows where he is."

Terry tried to calm Betty. He had no answers for her and he didn't know what to think.

Her sanity all but destroyed by his death Betty would not outlive Mario long. Following her death Terry became the guardian of the four Lanza children and brought them through childhood, adolescence and into adulthood. Scarred by the turbulence of their early lives, they nevertheless, under his guidance, reached their maturity, a firmly united family. Thanks to Terry's efforts the family estate has remained intact and the $200,000 annual royalties which are still received by the children from RCA Victor, twenty years after Lanza's death, have been wisely invested and guarantee their future security.

On October 21, two weeks after his death, Mario Lanza received his final funeral service. At Blessed Sacrament Church in Hollywood the copper casket was draped with an American flag. Movie moguls and stars mingled with fans—and the omnipresent photographers. Tony sobbed, "Leave my son. Take me. I'm old. Leave my son."

Only relatives and close friends were selected as pall-bearers. In Calvary Cemetery they bore Lanza to a temporary resting place. Later he and Betty were laid to rest in Holy Cross Cemetery.

Standing in the mob of celebrities, friends, and hangers-on, Terry thought how easy it would be for them to say they had known Mario Lanza. But they didn't really know him. Terry wasn't sure that even he did and he had seen Lanza in every possible mood. He thought of all the things they had gone through together. The feud with MGM, the nightmarish trip to New York when Mario was having a nervous break-down. In spite of the ups and downs, he had always treated Terry like a brother. Lanza's death was so unexpected, coming just when he was sounding happier and healthier than ever, that it was hard not to believe what Betty said. But Terry didn't want to think about that. So instead he thought all the way back to the day he had been working out in the gym and a young man had come up to him, and stuck out his hand, and said, "I'm Mario Lanza"; about the time he and George Eiferman had helped Mario and the pregnant Betty move into their new home and they had all joked about looking like a football team; about the first time Terry had ever sat in a recording studio and heard Mario sing and how it had made the hairs stand up on the back of his neck.

That was better, he thought; it made him feel better.

Appendix

MARIO LANZA
*Discography**

Friml: *The Vagabond King* (With Judith Raskin, Sop., Orch. cond. by Constantine Callinicos) Overture; Opening Chorus; Someday; Drinking Song; Love Me Tonight; Only a Rose; Tomorrow; Love for Sale; Hunting; Nocturne; Huguette Waltz; Song of the Vagabonds; Finale
LM/LSC-2509

The Desert Song; (Callinicos, Orch. and Cho.) Overture; Riff Song; Azuri's Dance; Instrumental; One Alone; (with Rasken, Sop.): The Desert Song; French Military Marching Song; Then You Will Know; Romance; One Good Boy Gone Wrong; (with Raskin, Sop.; Murcell, Bar.): I Want a Kiss; (with Arthur, Bass): Let Love Go; One Flower in Your Garden **LM/LSC-2440**

The Student Prince (Baron, Orch.) Overture; Golden Days; Thoughts Will Come Back To Me; Beloved (Brodszky-Webster); (And Cho.): Serenade; Drink, Drink, Drink; I'll Walk With God (Brodszky-Webster); Student Life; Gaudeamus Igitur; (with Giusti, Sop.): Summertime in Heidelberg (Brodszky-Webster); Just We Two (and Cho.); Deep in My Heart, Dear
LM/LSC-2339

Be My Love (Gold Standard Series) (Callinicos, Sinatra, Orch.) Be My Love with The Jeff Alexander Choir); Begin the Beguine (Porter); Night and Day (Porter); Song of India (Rimsky-Korsakoff) (and Cho.) **EPA-5047**

The Best of Mario Lanza (Brodszky-Cahn): Be My Love (RCA Victor Orch., Ray Sinatra, cond.; Jeff Alexander Choir), Because You're Mine (C. Callinicos at the Piano); And This Is My Beloved (Wright-Forrest) (Orch. cond. by Irving Aaronson; Jeff Alexander Choir); Funiculi' Funicula' (Denza) (Orch. and Cho. cond. by C. Callinicos); A Kiss (Brooks-Sinatra) (Orch. cond. by Ray Sinatra); One Alone (Romberg-Harbach-Hammerstein) (Orch. and Cho. cond. by C. Callinicos); Only a Rose (Friml-Hooker) (With Judith Raskin, Sop.;

Orch. cond. by C. Callinicos); The Loveliest Night of the Year (Aaronson-Webster-Rosas) (Orch. cond. by Ray Sinatra); Santa Lucia (Cottrau) (Orch. cond. by Paul Baron); Arrivederci Roma (Giovannini-Garinei-Rascel-Sigman) (From the MGM Film "The Seven Hills of Rome"); Pagliacci (Leoncavallo): Vesti la giubba (Orch. cond. by C. Callinicos); Serenade (Romberg-Donnelly) (Orch. and Cho. cond. by Paul Baron)
LM/LSC-2748(e)

Double Feature—Mario Lanza (From "That Midnight Kiss") (Callinicos, Orch.): La Boheme (Puccini): Act I: Che gelida manina; Mamma mia che vo' sape (Nutile-Russo); Core 'ngrato (Cardillo-Cordiferro); Celeste Aida (Verdi); (Sinatra, Orch.): I Know, I Know, I Know (Kaper-Russell); They Didn't Believe Me (Kern-Rourke); (From "Toast of New Orleans") (Callinicos, RCA Victor Orch. and Cho.): La Traviata (Verdi): Act I: Brindisi: Libiamo, libiamo, ne'lieti calici (with Malbin, Sop.); Madama Butterfly (Puccini): Act I: Love Duet: Stolta paura, l'amor (with Malbin, Sop.); L'Africana (Meyerbeer): Act IV: O Paradiso!; Carmen (Bizet): Act II: La fleur que tu m'avais jetee (Flower Song); Martha (Flotow): Act III: M'appari **LM-2422**

For the First Time (From the Soundtrack of the Corona Films production "For the First Time") (With Orch.) (Savina, Cond.): Come Prima (Panzeri-Taccani-Di Paola); Tarantella (Stoll); O sole mio (Di Capua); Neapolitan Dance (Stoll); O, mon amour (Je n'en connais pas la fin) (Asso-Monnot); Mazurka (Stoll); (Callinicos, Cond.): Pagliacci (Leoncavallo): Vesti la giubba; Otello (Verdi): Finale; Aida (Verdi): Act I; Ich liebe dich (Grieg); (Stoll, Cond.): Ave Maria (Schubert); (Rediske, Band): Hofbrauhaus Song (Wer einmal nur in Munchen war) (Bette-Hauff); Pineapple Pickers (Stoll)

LM/LSC-2338

★ RCA Victor Red Seal Albums

173

The Great Caruso (Callinicos, RCA Victor Orch.) Rigoletto (Verdi): Act I: Questa o quella, Act IV: La donna e mobile, Act II: Parmi veder le lagrime; Tosca (Puccini): Act I: Recondita Armonia, Act III: E lucevan le stelle; L'Elisir d'Amore (Donizetti): Act II: Una Furtiva lagrima; La Gioconda (Ponchielli): Cielo e marl; I Pagliacci (Leoncavallo): Act II: Vesti la giubba
LM/LSC-1127(e)

If You Are But A Dream (Sinatra, Orch.) April in Paris (from "Walk a Little Faster") (Harburg-Duke); Time on My Hands (from "Smiles") (Adamson-Youmans-Gordan): What Is This Thing Called Love? (from "Wake Up and Dream") (Porter); Charmaine (Rapee-Pollack); A Little Love, A Little Kiss (Silesu-Ross); If You Are But a Dream (Rubenstein-Jaffe-Fulton-Bonx); Play, Gypsies-Dance, Gypsies (from "Countess Maritza" (Kalman-Smith-Brammer-Grunwald); Where or When (from "Babes in Arms") (Rodgers-Hart); A Kiss in the Dark (from "Orange Blossoms") (Herbert-De Sylva); My Buddy (Kahn-Donaldson); (Schwartz-Dietz): You and the Night and the Music (from "Revenge with Music"), Alone Together (from "Flying Colors")
LM/LSC-2790(e)

I'll See You in My Dreams (Orch. Cond. by Ray Sinatra) Spring Is Here (Rodgers-Hart): With a Song In My Heart; Among My Souvenirs Leslie-Nicholls); Marcheta (Schertzinger); Memories (Kahn-Van Alstyne); Naughty Marietta (Young-Herbert): Ah! Sweet Mystery of Life; I'll Be Seeing You (Fain-Kahal); Cosi Cosa (Washington-Kaper-Jurmann); Lady of Spain (Reeves-Evans); La Spagnola (Dole-DiChiara); When Day Is Done (DeSylva-Katscher); Good News (DeSylva-Brown-Henderson): The Best Things in Life Are Free; I'll See You In My Dreams (Kahn-Jones)
LM/LSC-2720(e)

I'll Walk with God (with Orch.) (C. Callinicos, Cond.): Ave Maria (Bach-Gounod), Cavalleria Rusticana (Mascagni): Addio alla madre; (and Cho.): I'll Walk with God (Brodszky-Webster), The Virgin's Slumber Song (Reger), O Holy Night (Adam); (Ray Sinatra, Cond.): Somebody Bigger Than You and I (Lange-Heath-Burke), Because (Teschemacher-d'Hardelot), The Trembling of a Leaf (Lawrence-Green), None But the Lonely Heart (David-Hoffman-Livingston-Tchaikovsky), Through the Years (Heyman-Youmans), I Love Thee (Grieg), Trees (Kilmer-Rasbach), (and The Jeff Alexander Choir): The Lord's Prayer (Malotte), Guardian Angels (Marx-Gerda) (Harpo Marx, Harp)
LM-2607

I'll Walk With God (Gold Standard Series) (Callinicos, Orch. and Cho.): I'll Walk With God; (Orch., The Jeff Alexander Choir, Sinatra, Cond.): The Lord's Prayer; Guardian Angels (with Harpo Marx, Harp); (Callinicos, RCA Victor Orch.): Ave Maria (J. S. Bach-Gounod)
EPA-5048

"A Kiss," and Other Love Songs (Sinatra, Orch.) A Kiss (Sinatra); Begin the Beguine (Porter); Long Ago (Kern); The Night Is Young and You're So Beautiful (Suesse); My Heart Stood Still (Rodgers-Hart); Sylvia (Speaks); The Moon Was Yellow (Ahlert); Night and Day (Porter); My Romance (Rodgers-Hart); Siboney (Lecuona); The Thrill Is Gone (Brown-Henderson); Valencia (Padilla); Beautiful Love (Young); Yesterdays (Harbach-Kern); Besame Mucho (Valazquez); Without A Song (Youmans)
LM-1860

Lanza on Broadway (Aaronson, Orch.; The Jeff Alexander Choir) On the Street Where You Live (Loewe-Lerner); Younger Than Springtime (Rodgers-Hammerstein); Speak Low (Weill-Nash); More Than You Know (Youmans-Rose-Eliscu); Falling in Love with Love (Rodgers-Hart); Why Was I Born (Hammerstein-Kern); And This Is My Beloved (Wright-Forrest); So in Love (Porter); September Song (Weill-Anderson); My Romance (Rodgers-Hart); This Nearly Was Mine (Rodgers-Hammerstein); You'll Never Walk Alone (Rodgers-Hammerstein)
LM-2070

Lanza Sings Christmas Carols (Baron, Orch. and Cho.) The First Noel; O Come, All Ye Faithful (Adeste Fideles); Away in a Manger; We Three Kings of Orient Are; O Little Town of Bethlehem; Silent Night (Gruber); Deck the Halls; Hark! The Herald Angels Sing (Mendelssohn); God Rest Ye Merry, Gentlemen; Joy to the World (Handel); O Christmas Tree; I Saw Three Ships; It Came Upon a Midnight Clear; Guardian Angels
LM/LSC-2333

Love Songs and Neapolitan Serenade (RCA Victor Orch.) (with Constantine Callinicos, Cond.): Because (Teschemacher-d'Hardelot), For You Alone (O'Reilly-Geehl), Marechiare (Di Giacomo-Tosti), 'A Vucchella (d'Annunzio-Tosti), Serenade (Silvestri-Toselli), Serenade (Sturani-Drigo); (Ray Sinatra, Cond.): I Love Thee (Ich liebe dich) (Grieg), Mattinata (Leoncavallo), O sole mio (di Capua), My Song, My Love (Gerda-Beelby), Be My Love (Brodszky) (and Jeff Alexander Choir), I'll Never Love You (Cahn)
LM/LSC-1188(e)

Loveliest Night of the Year (Gold Standard Series) (Sinatra, Orch.): Siboney (Lecuona); Valencia (Padilla); Granada (Lara); (Callinicos, RCA Victor Orch.): The Loveliest Night of the Year
EPA-5083

Magic Mario (Sinatra, Orch.) The World Is Mine Tonight (Posford); Wanting You (Romberg); When You're in Love (C. Fischer); Parlami d'amore, Mariu (C. A. Bixio); Tell Me Tonight (Spoliansky); Softly As in a Morning Sunrise (Romberg); Fools Rush In (Bloom); One Alone (Romberg); None But the Lonely Heart (Tchaikovsky); Ay-Ay-Ay (Freire); The Trembling of a

174

Leaf (Green); Make Believe (Kern); Roses of Picardy (Wood) **LM-1943**

Mario! (With Orch. And Cho.) Funiculi' Funicula' (Turco-Denza); Dicitencello vuie (Falvo-Fusco); Maria Mari' (Russo-Di Capua); Voce 'e notte (Lardini-de Curtis); Canta pe' me (Bovio-de Curtis); O surdato 'namurato (Califano-Cannio); Come facette mammeta (Capaldo-Gambardella); Santa Lucia luntana (Mario); Fenesta che lucive (Ignoto); Tu ca nun chiagne (Bovio-de Curtis); 'Na sera 'e maggio (Pisano-Cioffi); Passione (Bovio-Tagliaferri-Valente **LM/LSC-2331**

Mario Lanza in a Cavalcade of Show Tunes (Rene Orch.; The Jeff Alexander Choir) Lover Come Back to Me (from "The New Moon") (Hammerstein-Romberg); I've Told Ev'ry Little Star (from "Music in the Air") (Hammerstein-Kern); The Donkey Serenade (from "The Firefly") (Friml); All the Things You Are (from "Very Warm for May") (Hammerstein-Kern); Giannina Mia (from "The Firefly") (Friml); Rose Marie (from "Rose Marie") (Hammerstein-Friml); Yours Is My Heart Alone (from "The Land of Smiles") (Lehar); Thine Alone (from "Eileen") (Herbert); Will You Remember (Sweetheart) (from "Maytime") (Romberg); Gypsy Love Song (Slumber On, My Little Gypsy Sweetheart) (from "The Fortune Teller") (Herbert); Only a Rose (from "The Vagabond King") (Friml); Tramp! Tramp! Tramp! (from "Naughty Marietta") (Herbert) **LM-2090**

Mario Lanza in "Serenade" La Danza (Rossini); Torna a Surriento (de Curtis); La Boheme (Puccini); Act I: O soave fanciulla (with Fenn, Sop.); Der Rosenkavalier (R. Strauss): Act I: Di rigori armato; L'Africana (Meyerbeer): Act III: O Paradiso; Ave Maria (Schubert) (with Organ); L'Arlesiana (Cilea): Lamento di Federico; Turandot (Puccini): Act III: Nessun dorma; (With Heindorf, Orch.): Serenade (Cahn-Brodszky); Il Trovatore (Verdi): Act III: Di quella pira; Fedora (Giordano): Act II: Amor ti vieta; Otello (Verdi): Act II: Dio ti Giocondi (with Albanese, Sop.), My Destiny (Cahn-Brodszky) **LM-1996**

Mario Lanza Program, A (With Constantine Callinicos at the Piano) L'Arlesiana (Cilea): Lamento di Federico; Gia, il sole del Gange (A. Scarlatti); Pieta, Signore (Stradella); Tell Me, Oh Blue, Blue Sky (Giannini); Bonjour, ma belle; (Behrend); The House on the Hill (Charles); Tosca (Puccini): E lucevan le stelle; Mamma mia, che vo' sape? (Nutile-Russo); 'A vucchella (Tosti-D'Annunzio); Marechiare (Tosti-Di Giacomo); I'm Falling in Love with Someone (Herbert-Young); Because You're Mine (Brodszky-Cahn); Seven Hills of Rome (Young-Adamson) **LM/LSC-2454**

Mario Lanza Sings Caruso Favorites (Baron, Orch.) Vieni sul mar; Senza nisciuno (DeCurtis-Barbieri); Musica proibita (Gastaldon); Vaghissima sembianza (Donaudy); Serenata (Caruso-Bracco); Lolita (Buzzi-Peccia); Luna d'estate (Tosti); L'Alba sopara dalla luce l'ombra (D'Annunzio-Tosti); Pour un baiser (Doncieux-Tosti); La mia canzone (Cimmino-Tosti); Ideale (Errico-Tosti); Santa Lucia **LM/LSC-2393**

Seven Hills of Rome Seven Hills of Rome (Adamson-Young); There's Gonna Be a Party Tonight (Stoll); Lolita (Buzzi-Peccia); Rigoletto (Verdi): Questa o quella; Arrivederci, Roma (Garinei-Giovannini-Stillman-Rascel); Imitation Sequence: Temptation (Brown), Jezebel (Shanklin), Memories Are Made of This (Gilkyson-Rich Dehr-Miller), When the Saints Go Marching In; Come Dance with Me (Blake-Leibert); Never Till Now (Webster-Green); (Rene, Orch.): Do You Wonder (Ray-Hill); Earthbound (Taylor-Richardson-Musel); Love in a Home (Mercer-DePaul); (Heindorf, Orch.): Serenade (Cahn-Brodszky); My Destiny (Cahn-Brodszky) **LM-2211**

The Touch of Your Hand (Sinatra, Orch.) The Touch of Your Hand (Harbach-Kern); The Song Is You (Hammerstein-Kern); Oh, Nights of Splendor (Neapolitan Nights) (Kerr-Zamecnik); Someday I'll Find You (Coward); Your Eyes Have Told Me So (Kahn-Alstyne-Blaufuss); Strange Music (Forrest-Wright); The Desert Song (Hammerstein-Harbach-Romberg); You Are Love (Hammerstein-Kern); Day In—Day Out (Mercer-Bloom); Love Is the Sweetest Thing (Noble); I'm Falling in Love with Someone (Young-Herbert); Look for the Silver Lining (De Sylva-Kern); I've Got You Under My Skin; The Hills of Home (Calhoun-Fox) **LM-1927**

You Do Something to Me (Callinicos, Orch.) You Do Something to Me (Porter); Sylvia (Ray Sinatra, Cond.); Some Day (Friml) (Ray Sinatra, Cond.); Beloved; Song of India (Rimsky-Korsakoff) (and Cho.); Lolita (Ray Sinatra, Cond.); You Are My Love (and Cho.); Lygia (Ray Sinatra, Cond.); Flower Song (from "Carmen") (Bizet); Che gelida manina (Your Tiny Hand Is Frozen) (from "La Boheme") (Puccini); O tu che in seno agli angeli (Thou Heavenly One) (from "La Forza del Destino") (Verdi) **CAL/CAS-450(e)**

LANZA, MARIO, Tenor
Christmas Hymns and Carols (With the Jeff Alexander Choir) (With Henri Rene's Orch.): Joy to the World (Handel), O Christmas Tree, Hark! The Herald Angels Sing (Mendelssohn), God Rest Ye Merry, Gentlemen, I Saw Three Ships; (With Orch, Ray Sinatra, Cond.): The Lord's Prayer (Malotte), O Come, All Ye Faithful (Adeste Fideles), Away in a Manger (Luther's Cradle Hymn), The First Noel, We Three Kings of Orient Are, O Little Town of Bethlehem, Silent Night (Gruber), Guardian Angels; O Holy Night (With RCA Victor Orch. and Cho., Constantine Callinicos, Cond.) **CAL/CAS-777(e)**

MARIO LANZA FAN CLUBS

Nicholas Petrella, President
The Mario Lanza Institute
1414 Snyder Avenue
Philadelphia, Pennsylvania 19145

Richard Gower, Executive Director
The Mario Lanza International Foundation
2027 Wayne Circle
Maryville, Tennessee 37801

Robert Dolfi, Secretary
Headquarters for
The Mario Lanza International Foundation
1840 South 4th Street
Alhambra, California 91801

Edith Kamin, President
Kreis Der Mario-Lanza Freund,
Pflogerstr. 24
1 Berlin, Germany 44

Pauline Franklin, Secretary
The British Mario Lanza Society
Flat 34 - St. John's Court
Calthorpe Road - Banbury
Oxon, England, OX168HS

INDEX

178

179